ADVANCED COACHING PRACTICE

Sara Miller McCune founded SAGE Publishing in 1965 to support the dissemination of usable knowledge and educate a global community. SAGE publishes more than 1000 journals and over 800 new books each year, spanning a wide range of subject areas. Our growing selection of library products includes archives, data, case studies and video. SAGE remains majority owned by our founder and after her lifetime will become owned by a charitable trust that secures the company's continued independence.

Los Angeles | London | New Delhi | Singapore | Washington DC | Melbourne

ADVANCED COACHING PRACTICE

INSPIRING CHANGE IN OTHERS

CHRISTIAN VAN NIEUWERBURGH
& DAVID LOVE

Los Angeles | London | New Delhi
Singapore | Washington DC | Melbourne

Los Angeles | London | New Delhi
Singapore | Washington DC | Melbourne

SAGE Publications Ltd
1 Oliver's Yard
55 City Road
London EC1Y 1SP

SAGE Publications Inc.
2455 Teller Road
Thousand Oaks, California 91320

SAGE Publications India Pvt Ltd
B 1/I 1 Mohan Cooperative Industrial Area
Mathura Road
New Delhi 110 044

SAGE Publications Asia-Pacific Pte Ltd
3 Church Street
#10-04 Samsung Hub
Singapore 049483

© Christian van Nieuwerburgh and David Love 2019

First published 2019

Editor: Susannah Trefgarne
Assistant editor: Talulah Hall
Production editor: Rachel Burrows
Copyeditor: Solveig Gardner Servian
Proofreader: David Hemsley
Indexer: David Rudeforth
Marketing manager: Samantha Glorioso
Cover design: Sheila Tong
Typeset by: C&M Digitals (P) Ltd, Chennai, India
Printed in the UK by Ashford Colour Press Ltd.

Library of Congress Control Number: 2018961437

British Library Cataloguing in Publication data

A catalogue record for this book is available from the British Library

ISBN 978-1-5264-2123-4
ISBN 978-1-5264-2124-1 (pbk)

At SAGE we take sustainability seriously. Most of our products are printed in the UK using responsibly sourced papers and boards. When we print overseas we ensure sustainable papers are used as measured by the PREPS grading system. We undertake an annual audit to monitor our sustainability.

Christian writes:
To Cathia, Christian and Tsuyu – for being there for me.

David writes:
To Alba, Tom, Sara, Ben and Pam – for bringing constant light and love into my life.

CONTENTS

ABOUT THE AUTHORS

Christian van Nieuwerburgh is an experienced executive coach, educational consultant and academic. He is the Executive Director of Growth Coaching International, a global provider of coach training for the education sector. Seen as a leading authority in the field of coaching, he has written numerous books and articles on the topic. Christian delivers keynote presentations and workshops internationally and teaches at a number of academic institutions. He is Professor of Coaching and Positive Psychology at the University of East London (UK), Visiting Professor at the University of Bergamo (Italy) and Honorary Fellow of the Centre for Positive Psychology at the University of Melbourne (Australia).

Christian is passionate about the use of coaching and positive psychology in education. He is particularly interested in exploring how coaching can be used to create ideal learning environments. He enjoys working with schools and individual coaching clients all over the world and has written about the concept of interculturally-sensitive coaching. When he is not teaching, supervising or leading teams of coaches, Christian likes to focus his attention on three things: spending time with loved ones; riding the world's most beautiful roads on a motorcycle; and taking time to think and write.

David Love is a qualified and experienced executive coach working with senior and middle managers in the NHS, local government and other public services. He has extensive experience of organisational, leadership and management development and assists public services to build and sustain coaching cultures. He is a trained and experienced coach supervisor, working with in-house coaches, for example, in NHS trusts. As an Associate Senior Fellow with the University of Birmingham's Institute for Local Government Studies (INLOGOV), David coaches aspiring chief executives of local authorities. He is a Visiting Tutor on Henley Business School's masters-level Professional Certificate in Coaching programme.

David is deeply committed to helping to improve outcomes for citizens through enabling senior managers to become better leaders through coaching. He is particularly interested in the place of learning in improving personal impact and performance and sees coaching as a highly effective way of blending organisational priorities with leadership learning. He works to build coachees' capacity to self-coach and use coaching approaches with their colleagues as one way of building cultures where individual and team learning contributes to improved service provision and business operations. David has a creative streak and uses cartooning, sketching and other visual thinking techniques in his coaching.

PROLOGUE

When we first sat down together to start thinking about this book, we were not entirely sure what the focus and content would be. In fact, in our first conversation, we weren't even sure that there was a book to write. In recent years the number of texts about coaching has mushroomed and we are lucky (as a profession) to have so many good publications to turn to. We were wondering what we had to offer that had not already been covered eloquently by the growing number of eminent writers in the field (of whom we are avid readers ourselves). One of us had already written a book about the core skills of coaching, so an 'advanced coaching skills' follow-up seemed a logical next step.

During that first meeting, we attempted to explore what 'advanced skills' in coaching were – and got stuck. We arrived at the conclusion that beyond the vital skills (such as contracting, open questioning, active listening and providing challenge) everything else is 'advanced'. And we grappled with the idea that a skill defined by one coach as 'advanced' might be seen by another coach as necessary.

The more we talked about it, the more the word 'skill' seemed problematic. Surely, we thought, successful coaching involves more than a set of skills, whether we call them foundational or advanced? As experienced coaches and continuing learners ourselves we wanted to make a unique and personal contribution that would interest and engage experienced coaches. This reminder of our purpose gave us energy and enthusiasm, and some essential underlying principles started to emerge.

We wanted our writing to be rooted in the practice of coaching – we both believe that we can only get better at coaching through practice and reflection. We wanted our thinking to draw on theoretical concepts as appropriate and to grow out of our own, and others', real-life coaching experiences.

As practitioners who are involved in facilitating the development and supervision of novice and experienced coaches, we notice the appetite in many people for more and more skills and models to add to their repertoires. While competencies (advanced or otherwise) and techniques are very important ingredients, we believe that successful coaching outcomes arise from a more nuanced and sophisticated 'coaching way of being', based on creating and sustaining powerful relationships.

We decided to use the process of writing as a way of learning. We feel confident that, if we are learning, there will be a good chance that other coaches reading this book would gain something too. This notion was liberating – we realised we could express our views and thinking without being overly committed to a particular coaching model or approach. We could be curious and fascinated with what emerged, and present this with honesty, openness and humility. And best of all, we could do this while enjoying the process.

It occurred to us that starting to write a book without a fixed idea of the content felt very similar to the coaching conversations that we frequently engage in. Coaches step into each uncharted coaching conversation with a firm belief that something helpful will emerge. As coaches ourselves, we are comfortable with the idea of 'emergence'. We trust that through the process of working together to consider real-life coaching practice, sharing, challenging and questioning one another's perspectives, interesting ideas, insights and learning will emerge.

We began by thinking about analogies that might offer insights into the coaching relationship and conversation. Driving a car seemed like a good starting point – and is a useful, and much-used analogy in the field. For example, Jonathan Passmore uses this analogy in his book, *Excellence in Coaching* (2015). As with coaching, when we first learn to drive, we have to get to grips with the basic practicalities of the craft. Pressing the clutch to the floor while manipulating the gearstick and checking the rear-view mirror all feel tricky at first – like listening well, thinking of questions to ask and paying attention to the coachee in a coaching conversation. After practice, these disparate skills merge into a holistic entity and the process of driving (or coaching) becomes second nature as unconscious competence comes into play and we can travel hundreds of miles safely. Hopefully with more practice and experience we become more proficient, only becoming consciously incompetent again when we encounter a new event (for example, driving a hire car in a new country).

This analogy works well as a description of the early stages of becoming a coach. While a few of us move on to take an advanced driving skills course to enhance our competence, most drivers rely on their initial training and their increasing hours behind the wheel for their proficiency. So what would be a better analogy for advanced coaching practice? Sport is another much-used source of possibilities, especially given that coaching is such an inherent feature. Tim Gallwey helpfully uses the example of tennis to help coaches think about/focus on the crucial psychological features (the 'inner game') in play in a coaching conversation (1975). However, while coaching is like tennis in many respects, it is not competitive, and one does not emerge a winner while the other loses.

One of us is a keen photographer. In the constant quest for great photographs he has attended workshops and courses, voraciously consumed articles and books, and bought ever-more technically advanced cameras. While additional learning does not go amiss, neither this nor bigger and better equipment gives a guarantee of success. The photographer Ibarionex Perello writes:

> … the ability to consistently make the 'great' photograph seemed elusive. … I was simply pointing my camera at people, places and things and 'documenting' them. The image looked just like the object that had drawn my attention, but there was little else there – none of what I *felt* while making the image, especially not the excitement I had experienced.
>
> What was it that finally allowed me to produce the kind of images I aspired to readily and consistently create? The answer was a simple one: I started paying attention to what was happening to the light. (2011: 4)

What emerges as crucial to a powerful image then, is an awareness of the intricate interplay of light on the subject of the photograph. Similarly in coaching, it is our belief that selecting the 'right model' as the lens for viewing the topic is less important than noticing the detail of what is happening with and around the coachee.

With these analogies in mind, we are looking forward to contributing to the understanding of what constitutes advanced coaching practice. Our intention is to support experienced coaches by exploring the complexities and depth of coaching practice. As a result, this resource will:

- focus on the practicalities of real-life coaching
- provide access to videos of coaching practice
- share reflections based on our own coaching
- draw on a range of relevant research-informed theories
- challenge readers' thinking.

We want this book to support your personal exploration of coaching. We are acutely aware of the fact that there is never one version of reality. As two authors, we will make different contributions to this endeavour. We are energised by the thought that there is never one right answer. This allows us to make choices all the time about how to best guide our coachees through conversations, jettisoning numerous other potential avenues of possibility in the process. So, as authors we are likely to notice different things and hold potentially opposing views. You, the experienced coach, will bring your own perspective into play. You may agree or disagree with what you read, and you will notice things that we have missed. That is what makes this project so exciting for us. We hope that this will be a journey of reflexivity for us all.

ACKNOWLEDGEMENTS

CHRISTIAN AND DAVID WRITE

There's a danger that what follows begins to sound like one of those lengthy acceptance speeches at the Oscars. Given that it's in print you will at least be spared seeing those moments when our emotions overwhelm us! No doubt when we both read this after publication we will remember other people we should have mentioned.

We would like to start by expressing our immense gratitude to the coaches who gave up their valuable time to be videoed working with coachees as a starting point for our book. In addition to the extracts from these coaching conversations that accompany the book they also took part in videoed debrief interviews, which have contributed to shaping our thinking about advanced practice. For their invaluable contributions we thank Helen Brown, Jackee Holder, Denis Sartain and Bob Thomson.

Others who gave their time to help create the coaching videos were, of course, the coachees. For enabling the videoed conversations to be about real people and live issues we are extremely grateful to Lina Ashour, Diana Franco, Robin Lupton, Georgia Patey, Clare Spencer and Nazim Uddim.

Finally, we have greatly appreciated the support we have received from those at SAGE Publishing in bringing our book to fruition, particularly Robert Berry, Rachel Burrows, Amy Jarrold, Talulah Hall, Susannah Trefgarne and Claire Williams.

CHRISTIAN WRITES

I am grateful to many people who have provided encouragement and support. The process of working on this book has provided many opportunities to discuss coaching with respected colleagues and friends. Some leading academics in the field of coaching have been very kind to me, acting as mentors and advisers at key moments in my professional life. I'd like to particularly thank Tatiana Bachkirova, Robert Biswas-Diener, Anthony Grant, Suzy Green, Alison Hardingham, Peter Hawkins, Stephen Joseph, Lindsay Oades, Jonathan Passmore, Gordon Spence, Tim Theeboom, Bob Thomson, Mary Watt and Julia Yates.

During the period of writing this book, I've become more involved with Growth Coaching International (GCI), a specialist coach training provider for the education sector. I'm grateful to everyone involved in that organisation. The opportunity to work with like-minded, generous and passionate people is very much appreciated. I'd like to particularly thank the management and administrative team for being so welcoming: Philip Bell, Deirdre Brigden, Kathleen Cash, Ainsley Chadwick, Elly De La Rue Browne, Jess Joils, Debbie Knoke, Alex Kupsik-Jankowska, Nancy Morley, Tanya Prentice and Clare Sturrock. GCI has an amazing team of facilitators, coaches and consultants, and I cannot wait to work more closely with them. I've enjoyed all my interactions with the team. I am especially thankful for the advice, support and encouragement of Annette Gray, Diane Henning, Jan Hill, Grant O'Sullivan, Kerry Mitchell, Kris Needham, Gray Ryan and Penny Verdich. The emerging partnership between GCI and the Instructional Coaching Group has allowed me to work closely with two people who I consider to be role models of the coaching way of being – John Campbell and Jim Knight. Both are highly valued professional colleagues and personal friends. I'm also grateful to Vicki Campbell and Jenny Knight who have been wonderfully supportive.

While writing this book, I've been involved in a number of writing projects with Margaret Barr and Chris Munro. They are both thoughtful, kind and valued friends and colleagues. I also learn so much when I co-facilitate workshops with Ben Calleja, Claudia Owad and Jason Pascoe. Conversations with these GCI colleagues are always enriching and insightful. I have also been fortunate to interact with amazing colleagues and clients through my work with The Coach House. Helen Tiffany is an inspiring leader, executive coach and colleague, and it's a pleasure to work with Joanna Head and Stephanie Clements of the Bec Development team.

The University of East London (UEL) is my academic home. I'm lucky to work with supportive colleagues at this institution. I am particularly grateful to Cressida Campbell, Rose Cole, Liam Cookson, Yannis Fronimos, Kevin Head, Mark Holloway, Vanessa Koonjul, Nash Popovic, Shama Shah, Minal Shingadia, Guy Tamlyn and Aneta Tunariu. I'm a member of the academic team on the MSc in Applied Positive Psychology and Coaching Psychology at UEL. I'd like to thank the amazing people on the team: Jolanta Burke, Kirsty Gardiner, Andrea Giraldez, Rosie Hancock, Rona Hart, Kate Hefferon, Hanna Kampman, Tim Lomas, Julia Papworth, William Pennington, Pradnya Surana and Cecilia Yardley.

Much of my learning about coaching happens when I'm with engaged students. I am grateful to the students that I have had the pleasure of working with at the University of

East London, Henley Business School (University of Reading), Anglia Ruskin University and the University of Bergamo. I am energised and more hopeful when I have the opportunity to meet passionate educators, so I am thankful for the interactions that I have had with teachers and school leaders at conferences and workshops all over the world. Thank you for being such inspirational educators! I would also like to acknowledge the participants of the 'Advanced Coaching Practice' workshop at the Teaching, Learning, Coaching Conference in Las Vegas in October 2018 and participants at a workshop at the West Midlands Coaching and Mentoring Pool Conference in December 2018. With a group of about 24 experienced US-based coaches and about 60 experienced UK-based coaches, I had the opportunity to share some of the ideas that are presented in this book. Their full engagement, thoughtful interactions and real-life examples were very helpful.

Of course, none of this would be as enjoyable without the love and support of my family. I am grateful to my mother, Tsuyu Tsuchida, who has been a source of inspiration all of my life. Cathia Jenainati is my life partner and her love and companionship mean the world to me. Our son, Christian Arthur van Nieuwerburgh, is a constant source of joy and pride. The Jenainati family has embraced me as one of their own, and it's wonderful to be part of such a caring and loving community.

Everyone mentioned above has had a role in supporting me to do the best job possible in writing this book. Finally, I'd like to express my thanks to David Love, my co-author. He is the one who first introduced me to the art and craft of coaching. He was and continues to be an excellent teacher of coaching and the coaching way of being! I count myself fortunate to have had the opportunity to interact with and learn from so many wonderful people.

DAVID WRITES

There are so many people to thank. Colleagues, friends and family who have contributed in significant ways to my development as a coach. First, there are my very experienced coaching colleagues, particularly the members of the OPM Coaching Supervision Group in its various guises, who over many years have shared (confidentially of course) their observations, obstacles and achievements in their coaching practice: Bob Baker, Helen Brown, Lesley Campbell, Stefan Cantore, Sue Goss, Helen Ferris, Richard Field, Liz Goold, Anita Grabarz, Tamsin Hewitt, Alison Hodge, Claire Lazarus, Munira Thobani, Hilary Samson-Barry, Hilary Thompson, Tim Whitworth and Jude Williams.

I am also extremely grateful to the expert supervisors connected with this supervision group over the years: Jenny Bird, Sarah Goldsworthy, Alison Hodge and Gil Schwenk, who have all supported and challenged my growth as a coach. Sarah continues this process with me on a one-to-one basis and as a consummate supervisor can always be relied on to help generate vital insights into my practice. I leave every session with her a more enlightened practitioner.

There are other colleagues from OPM (Office for Public Management, now Traverse) too numerous to mention who stretched my leadership and organisational development capabilities during my 13 years with the organisation. I am particularly grateful for their enduring patience with a confirmed introvert in a very extraverted world. Those I worked with closely include Sophie Ahmad, Peta Barnes, Anne Bennett, David Bryan, Sheba Cheung, Elaine Clough, Simon Courage, Jude Cummins, Robin Douglas, Anna Eliatamby, Ewan King, Yee-Mai Koo, Hywel Lloyd, Paul Lloyd, Catherine Mangan, Andrew Mann, Clive Miller, Jasmine Miller, Greg Parston, Jonathan Passmore, Ian Roberts, Deborah Rozansky, Sonal Shah, Shannon Shuemake, Paul Tarplett, Carol Ward, Sonia Watson and Sharon Wright.

I first met Andrena Cumella at OPM and we continue to work together on coaching-related projects. She has contributed helpful insights to this book and I am exceedingly thankful for her enduring wisdom, humour and camaraderie. Another long-standing connection from my OPM days is with Anna Eliatamby whose commitment to communalism, courage in her work in warzones and generosity of thinking remains a source of support and inspiration.

I had no way of seeing it at the time but in the first stages of my career, as an advice and community worker in the 1970s, the foundations for my coaching work were being laid. For example, learning how to listen carefully to the details of a complicated welfare rights problem in an office bustling with other activity honed my listening skills. I am immensely grateful to the people I worked with and met during this formative time, who opened my eyes to the power of concerted collective action to improve people's lives: Liz Alderton, Agnes Alexander, Dany Baker, Phil Baker, Frances Barnett, Simon Brown, Kaz Burek, Marion East, Dave Ellis, Sara Grossman, Colin Langton, Vera Mitchell, Alan Stanton, Marie-Francoise Tollemer and Jonathan and Sushila Zeitlyn.

Ten years with the team at Pathway working on communication and race equality matters in organisations was another formative period for me. For their unswerving commitment and insights I am indebted to Phil Baker, Sheila Cogill, Daphne Crossfield, Denise Gubbay, Zahida Hussain, Amarjit Khera, Helen Marchington, Jane Saunders, Arvind Sharma, Jaswinder Sidhu and Pete Wilson from whom I learnt so much about organisational consultancy, equality, and how to work effectively with powerful issues.

As a senior and middle manager in further education colleges I built a grounding in leadership and management (I wish I'd known then what I know now!) thanks mainly to Sandra Chalmers, Arvind Sharma, and Hilary and Ian Wallis.

I know that I learn from every encounter with coachees and the coaches I supervise and teach. I therefore thank all those people over the last 15 years with whom I have had the privilege to work. I have also had the pleasure of working with numerous public service organisations to assist with their ambitions to build coaching cultures. Again, aside from the core purpose of the work (obviously the most important factor!) these have been tremendous learning opportunities for me, for which I am extremely grateful. Particular thanks go to clients with whom I have long-standing relationships: Petra Bryan, Fiona

Ibberson and the coaches of the in-house Pennine Care NHS Foundation Trust coaching team; Sam Darby, Rebecca Davis and the coaches of West Midlands Coaching and Mentoring Pool; Suzy Taylor and Hendrix Timu of NHS Improvement; Samantha Peterson of NHS Business Services Authority; and Joe Ann Rushton, Tresa Andrews, Emma Balfe, Amynta Cardwell and Marcus Maguire of Central & North West London NHS Foundation Trust.

Over the years, and particularly since becoming a freelance executive coach, I have had the pleasure of working with a number of impressive coaches, facilitators and consultants on development-related activities. I have learnt much from these collaborators who include: Sarah Akroyd (The Centre for Mentoring and Coaching), Peter Birch (The Talking Edge), Bill Crooks (Mosaic Creative), Daniel Goodwin (Daniel Goodwin Ltd), Chris Lawrence-Pietroni (Leading Communities), Damian Gaskin (The Forum Partnership), Barrie Smale (Inspired2Learn), Michael Spooner (Pansophia Business Innovation) and Pankajroy Dalwadi (Nisus Ltd).

I also wish to extend my thanks to my new colleagues at Henley Business School's Professional Certificate in Coaching programme, who are already stimulating practice-based reflections and insights: Tracy Barr, Julia Carden, Alison Hardingham, Ann James, Jonathan Passmore and Tatiana Rowson.

Clearly coaching is informed by our experiences beyond the professional sphere. I am immensely grateful for the many hours of conversations about life in general with friends, which have, without doubt, contributed to my approach to coaching. My dad, if he were still with us, would describe such conversations as 'putting the world to rights'. For bringing richness to my life I thank Chris Haskett, Julia Holmes, Sue Jarvis, Ian Martin, Vera and Kim Mitchell, David Reading, and Rich, Marion, Amy and Peter Seal. In a similar vein I want to express immense appreciation to my family who give me unconditional encouragement, nurture my creativity and are the rock for my engagement with the wider world. Their unstinting support is invaluable, not least on those occasions when I become single-minded and inwardly focused on an activity – such as writing a book. Thank you Martyn, Julienne, Lauren and Daniel (my brother and family); Freda (my mother); Cic, Bob, Rachel, Peter, Ann and Phil (the Thorpe side); Kathie, David, Judy and David (the 'in-laws'); Bernie (my son's partner); Pam (my lifelong partner and pole star); as well as the truly inspirational Tom (my son), Sara (my daughter), Alba (my grand-daughter) and Ben Brown (Sara's partner).

Last, but not least, I wish to thank Christian. First for inviting me to join him in writing the follow-up to his *An Introduction to Coaching Skills* book. Then for the huge amount I have learnt from him in this project both through his intellectual support and the challenge to my thinking and practice, as well as about the writing process itself. We have also had a great deal of fun together getting from a blank sheet of paper, via numerous sticky notes and flipcharts, and many satisfying hours of conversation, to the printed publication. Our many humorous email and verbal exchanges loosely captured under the title 'Janet and John Go Coaching' may yet prove to be our next literary collaboration.

ONLINE RESOURCES

WATCH VIDEO CLIPS OF REAL-LIFE COACHING CONVERSATIONS BY EXPERIENCED PRACTITIONERS

Visit https://study.sagepub.com/advancedcoaching
While there are an increasing number of publications about coaching, there are relatively few opportunities for coaches to have a fly-on-the-wall perspective of what happens in real coaching conversations. Coaching supervision, of course, helps bring coaching conversations alive and is an essential source of reflection and insights for coaches. From our own supervision and development work with novice and experienced coaches we know there is an appetite to 'see behind the closed door' of the coaching space. This is why we often include coaching demonstrations in development programmes, where we coach a volunteer and enable the group to explore what they have seen. One insight that often results from this group analysis is the obvious, but nonetheless powerful insight that there are as many (and more) potential ways of approaching the conversation than there are people in the room. In places, we use the video as a starting point for discussion of advanced practice, and in others it is used to illustrate a particular aspect of practice. This symbol will point you to each relevant video.

1
THE COMPLEXITY OF ADVANCED COACHING PRACTICE

Coaching is a complex craft. When it works successfully for the coachee, it involves a set of sophisticated interactions which take place between two people engaged in a time-bound relationship. While the formal conversation takes place, a parallel series of thoughts and interconnections are arising separately for both coach and coachee. Each person has her own thought processes about the conversation and emotions associated with those thoughts. In addition, the interaction with the other person will be triggering further thoughts and emotions. Some of this internal complexity surfaces overtly into the coaching conversation. Some of it makes its way into the conversation through 'leakage'. Some thoughts and emotions will remain hidden to the other party altogether.

At its core, coaching is based on a set of relatively straightforward and easily learned skills (van Nieuwerburgh, 2017). At the same time, the most effective coaching takes these capabilities to their highest level, and then moves beyond them into territory that is focused on sustaining strong, meaningful and productive relationships. The coach must employ these high-level skills, manage her own thoughts and emotions *and* notice nuanced subtleties in how the coachee 'is' in the room. Mary Beth O'Neill (2007) has argued that effective coaches must demonstrate 'fearless compassion'. This is understood as having the confidence, presence and ability to focus on what needs to be challenged in order for the coachee to grow while 'holding' her in the safe and secure place that enables that exploration and growth to occur. Given that executive coaching is focused on improving the effectiveness of leaders, managers and other professionals in their work roles, the complexity of what is happening between coach and coachee is further complicated by the need to take into account organisational and wider systemic contexts.

In this book, we explore what makes coaching successful, and crucially, how coaches need to *be* to achieve that success. A useful place to start thinking is the trajectory coaches follow in gaining and honing their capabilities. Professional bodies in the coaching field have each established useful competency frameworks. For example, the ICF model includes a self-assessment process that encourages coaches to reflect on their current level of capability. While competency frameworks can be helpful, they are designed to provide a standard for coach behaviour and therefore can feel fixed. By their nature, such frameworks are less able to accommodate differences in style, approach and practice. In other words, competency-based frameworks are useful to establish whether a coach meets agreed professional standards but are not suited for assessing the complexity of advanced practice. It is difficult to capture and assess the ongoing and individualised growth that coaches experience as they become increasingly proficient. Peter Hawkins and Nick Smith (2013) make a valuable contribution to this debate by identifying a set of developmental levels that coaches move through as their capability grows.

Table 1.1   The development steps of a coach

Stage	Focus	Pre-occupations of coach
1	Self	'Can I make it in this work?'
2	Client	'Can I help this client make it?'
3	Process	'How are we relating together?'
4	Process-in-context	'How do processes interconnect?'

Source: Adapted from Hawkins & Smith, 2006: 139

Table 1.1 shows the steps of development of a coach. In the first stage, the coach's focus is on herself and she is primarily concerned about making the coaching process work while thinking about which models might be most effective. The second stage is characterised by an interest in the coachee with the intention of helping her to identify an action plan. The coaching process becomes a major consideration at stage three. The coach's attention turns to how the conversational process is affecting the relationship. The final stage involves the coach becoming much more aware of the context in which the coachee operates. The coach starts to reflect on how the coaching connects to other processes in the outside world. Viewed in this way, it becomes clear that part of a coach's development is building confidence in her own skill so that she is better able to attend to the needs of the coachee and her context.

As the focus of this book is on advanced coaching practice, we think it is helpful to explore the concept of developmental stages in a way that incorporates the complexity rather than take a linear perspective. The challenge is finding a way of discussing coach learning and growth without being limited to stages of development. Our intention, therefore, is to identify what we believe are the main elements of coach learning and growth. We will present this as an organic and dynamic process (see Figure 1.1) that includes phases as well as an appreciation that proficiency may be individual and the recognition that development does not always manifest itself in clearly identifiable and synchronised steps.

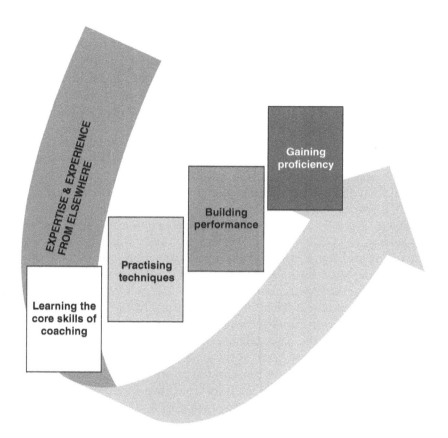

Figure 1.1   Phases in coach learning and growth

PHASE 1: LEARNING THE CORE SKILLS

People new to the role of coach encounter the core skills of contracting, open questioning, active listening and supportive challenge. In this initial phase, the focus is primarily centred on one's self. The coach tends to be preoccupied with learning and applying the core skills. At this level, the novice coach is like a learner driver undertaking a number of actions that may feel disjointed at first. In our coaching development and supervision work, we find that using open questions can be experienced as problematic by novice coaches. This results in coaches reverting to using closed or leading questions. For some, it can take a good deal of practice to make the necessary shift, despite an intellectual understanding that open questioning techniques can be more appropriate and powerful.

Similarly, novice coaches can quickly grasp the idea that active listening is important but in practice they can struggle to translate this intellectual understanding into their coaching. This experience can call into question the extent to which they *really* listen to their colleagues in everyday life. Paying detailed attention to what someone is saying is not always an easy task – especially in busy and dynamic environments. Other people's words may trigger relevant or seemingly irrelevant thoughts that can be distracting. Alternatively, they might be waiting for their chance to intervene, busily crafting responses to what is being said. For those attempting to listen as coaches, this 'inner voice' has the additional role of providing a commentary on the coaching process. It can support the coach's continual search for *the* insightful question to ask next. Ironically, of course, the internal chatter can actively disrupt attempts to listen effectively, which in turn reduces the chance that a helpful coaching question will arise from what the coachee is actually saying. Typically, new coaches are introduced to a simple and effective coaching process such as the GROW model (Whitmore, 1992), which provides a very helpful way of structuring and signposting a coaching conversation. The GROW process is easy to remember and deploy, creating a logical series of steps to enable the coachee to explore a topic. The popular acronym stands for Goal, Reality, Options and Will (GROW). However, using the model can elicit another question in the novice coach's inner dialogue: 'Where are we now in the GROW process?'

In this phase (learning the core skills), a novice coach may feel that contracting is a formal process that should only occur at the start of a series of coaching sessions. When contracting is undertaken, it can be delivered in a formulaic and transactional way. The novice coach will deploy the core skills of coaching intentionally and consciously. However, creating the appropriate balance of support and challenge can feel artificial to the coach, with the challenge element being given less priority. At this point, it is likely that novice coaches will be introduced to the concept of coaching supervision during their initial development programme. However, until the novice coach has more experience, the benefits of supervision may not be fully appreciated or realised.

PHASE 2: STRENGTHENING SKILLS AND TECHNIQUES

Like all crafts, coaching capability only improves with practice. Effective coach development programmes include opportunities to practise from the very start and encourage reflective practice through the use of diaries and journals. Beyond her initial training, the coach practises with real coachees. Through this it is recognised that while the basic features of coaching sessions remain largely the same, no two conversations are alike. A coach may think 'I've come across this issue before...' but realise that differing contexts and personalities mean that the conversations and outcomes will vary.

With practice the novice coach begins to integrate the core skills, creating stronger coherence between active listening and question generation. She finds her own way of covering the initial contracting so that this part of the process starts to feel more relaxed and natural. Indeed, there is a growing realisation of the importance of ongoing and regular contracting to ensure that the coaching goals remain pertinent and the relationship between the coach and coachee continues to be productive.

In this phase, the coach becomes adept with the GROW process and more confident in its use. Often, it is at this point that the coach becomes increasingly comfortable with moving backwards and forwards through the various stages of the process. Similar to the novice car driver who may have integrated clutch and gear changes into a smooth movement, it can become second nature. With this emerging confidence comes an ability to experiment with the GROW process and implement it flexibly in service of the coachee.

The novice coach may have been introduced to a number of coaching processes in her initial development programme and will practise using different techniques in her coaching. The coach continues to be primarily preoccupied with her own performance and is now making decisions about appropriate coaching processes to use with particular coachees. In our experience, this phase (strengthening skills and techniques) is also characterised by a strong desire to maintain the 'purity' of the coaching philosophy. For example, novice coaches may say things like 'I'm putting on my mentoring hat now' in order to allow themselves to step outside the coach role to make suggestions, provide personal experience or give advice.

Through practice, the coach improves her ability to craft constructive questions that introduce appropriate challenge into coaching conversations. With increasing hours of practice, the coach's focus begins to shift from her own preoccupations about the 'mechanics' of coaching to the needs and interests of the coachee. At this stage, supervision has become an important aspect of the coach's development. It is likely that the coach is undertaking facilitated supervision in groups and networking with peers.

PHASE 3: FOCUSING ON PERFORMANCE

In this phase, the coach feels confident in her competence and has developed sufficient experience to support her sense that she *can* coach. Up to now, her coaching may have tended to focus on helping coachees to solve problems and to establish action points for the implementation of solutions. Through reflective practice, the coach is becoming adept at empathic listening and is using the detail of what the coachee is saying as the basis for powerful questions.

While the coach will recognise that there is much more to learn, she no longer sees herself as new to coaching and is now capable of using a range of coaching techniques. She has become significantly more concerned with the coachee's needs, interests and aspirations and pays increasing attention to the organisational factors relevant to the coachee's agenda. As a result, the coach can be described as client-focused, placing significance on the building and maintenance of constructive coaching relationships. This is a timely development given Erik de Haan's research (2008), which underlines the importance of the coach–coachee relationship as *the* key factor in successful coaching.

The coach is also keen to add coaching techniques to her expanding repertoire in order to find novel ways of facilitating the coachee's thinking and learning. This appetite for new techniques promulgates a further set of choices for the coach. She now has to decide which of her portfolio of processes and techniques to use with a particular coachee, and how to introduce it into the conversation. The coach's over-riding concern in this phase tends to be about the coachee's performance so there is more focus on supporting the coachee to identify and commit to action. Underpinning this preoccupation are questions for the coach about how she and the coachee are relating and what is working in the coaching relationship. With increasing experience and a stronger focus on the coachee, the coach's interest in the impact of difference comes more into the foreground. Noticing how these differences impact her relationship with the coachee and the latter's relationships with others in her organisation starts to become a resource that can support progress towards the agreed coaching goals. The quality of the coaching alliance will be discussed in supervision. The opportunity to be supervised is valued by the coach and is now a regular part of the coach's reflective practice. At this stage of her development (focusing on performance), she may be working one-to-one with a coach supervisor.

PHASE 4: GAINING PROFICIENCY

With increased competence and confidence based on extended experience of coaching, the coach's attention moves towards the possibility of transformation. She is looking beyond the immediate issues brought to the session by the coachee. Simply addressing these by using a problem-solving approach is no longer considered sufficient. Now she is noticing helpful or unhelpful patterns in the coachee's thinking, emotions and behaviour that might be having an impact on outcomes. In this phase, the coach is concerned with how the collaborative endeavour transforms the way the coachee thinks, feels and behaves. An ever-growing interest in the specific impacts of diverse personalities, backgrounds, experiences and expertise informs each coaching encounter and the coach is increasingly comfortable with drawing on facets of difference to build the coachee's personal resources, insights and learning.

The coach pays more attention to noticing how the coachee 'is' in the room and points out any observed congruence and discrepancy between, for example, the words being used and body language. She has also become more confident in drawing on the 'evidence in the room' to create constructive challenge. Using the realities of the coaching relationship, including her own reactions to the coachee's thinking, emotions and behaviour, she enables powerful insights in the coachee. The coach is now more comfortable with the ways in which her own personal experience can be a resource for the coachee. She is able to integrate feedback about her own perceptions of the coachee and include stories from her own professional experience into the coaching process. While she may be sensitive in her contracting about bringing these aspects into the conversation, she no longer has need for a 'mentoring hat'.

Alongside a more holistic, person-centred view of the coachee as an individual, the coach has greater interest in the organisational context of the coachee. This leads to the coach being interested in how the coachee and the organisation affect each other's performance. The intricate interplay of personal and organisational factors allows the coach to attend to the impact of the coaching in a broader arena. Coaching supervision is the ideal place for exploring the complexities that emerge during such conversations. At this stage (gaining proficiency), supervision is considered central to the coach's way of working.

BEYOND PROFICIENCY

We have argued that the development of coaches may not always be a linear process. While we believe that this framework can be used to understand and support current practice, some questions remain unanswered. For example, the majority of coach training currently available tends to focus on building coaching capability and enhancing skills. However, it is generally agreed that coaches should continually improve their practice. If that is the case, what should happen after a coach becomes proficient? Perhaps coaches can intentionally focus on developing their 'way of being'? Or should they try to develop a particular quality of presence that can be powerful in coaching relationships? Or might it be more helpful to focus on increasing their self-awareness? Or might coaches start to broaden their learning from other disciplines? Or would it be better if coaches enhanced their effectiveness by thinking about power dynamics? How can coaches be confident in their abilities while remaining humble? What role does creativity play in transformative coaching practice? Should coaches be thinking more deeply about their impact on coachees' organisations and the wider system?

Some say that beyond proficiency is 'advanced practice' or 'mastery'. But what exactly do these terms mean? Are there 'advanced practices' that can be isolated and taught to proficient coaches? If these are important practices, why have proficient coaches not encountered them already? To what extent is coaching a craft, or is it more of an art? And what is mastery? Can one ever 'master' coaching? And what about the power dynamics and gender assumptions implied in that term? These and other questions about the ways in which coaches can develop have encouraged us to start exploring the complexity of advanced coaching practice. In the following chapters we will explore key aspects of advanced practice based on our own experiences, videos of experienced coaches, the recommendations of professional associations, relevant academic research and the work of other writers.

Figure 1.2

2
BEING FOCUSED ON PROCESS AND PRIORITISING THE RELATIONSHIP

Visit https://study.sagepub.com/advancedcoaching to watch the video discussed in this chapter:

VIDEO 2.1: Using own experience productively for the benefit of the coachee

One of the key aspects that makes coaching different from other types of conversation is the process that coaches and coachees engage in together. It is the role of the coach to provide clear structure and direction to the conversation, enabling the coachee to open up and extend her thinking in new and innovative ways. The process adopted by the coach may be made overt, or it may remain relatively hidden to the coachee. It provides a framework for facilitating a coachee's exploration without her having to be concerned about the process itself. In the coaching field, this attention to process has led to a multiplicity of helpful techniques for managing a productive route into and through conversations. John Whitmore's ubiquitous GROW model (1992) is an outstanding example of this.

Understandably, the novice coach focuses on learning about an effective conversational process as an essential ingredient in the craft of coaching. In our work as developers and supervisors of new coaches, we frequently find an almost insatiable desire to acquire 'more models' in the belief that additional tools will, of themselves, create better coaching outcomes. Clearly, it is helpful for coaches to be able to draw on a diverse array of processes in order to be responsive to their coachees' needs and interests. However, there is a risk that a novice coach becomes overly attentive to the process in a way that may interfere with the effectiveness of the coaching conversation. Until experience builds her confidence in using coaching techniques, the novice coach can find that attempting to call to mind the next stage in a coaching process causes her attention to drift away from engaging fully with her coachee. Conversely, in advanced practice, the coaching process remains crucially important but becomes second nature and takes a back seat as the coach pays attention to creating and sustaining the relationship with her coachee. The advanced practitioner notices what is happening to the quality of the relationship moment by moment. In fact, Douglas McKenna and Sandra Davis' (2009) analysis of the ingredients that lead to the success of one-to-one therapeutic relationships shows that the quality of the relationship accounts for 30 per cent of the impact of the conversation, compared to 15 per cent for the process.

The process a coach uses to work effectively with her coachee is clearly an important part of the mix. In the coaching videos produced for this book, we can see that experienced practitioners work with the complex interconnectivity of process and relationship, and the tensions that can exist between them. How does the experienced coach build and maintain effective working relationships quickly with her coachee? How does she judge that a particular technique will prove fruitful for the coachee even if its use may create discomfort and place strain on their relationship?

In this chapter we explore the question of maintaining an appropriate focus on process while placing the relationship at the centre of coaching. In a later chapter (Chapter 3: Being challenging and letting things go) we will return to focus on the quality of the relationship as a key determinant of when and how to challenge.

Reflections from experienced coaches: Prioritising the relationship

Investing time in the relationship

During a coaching supervision session, one experienced coach explains that he spends a significant amount of time in the first part of the conversation encouraging the coachee to talk about the detail of the topic under discussion. He does this in order to build a strong relationship with the coachee. Even though he is an experienced coach, he continues to use the GROW process because it provides a helpful and simple structure for the coaching conversation. It is his experience over many years that has given him faith in the process. 'I never know where the conversation is going but I know it will be OK', he says. He believes that his trust in the process will build a strong working relationship with the coachee and that, in turn, this relationship is more likely to lead to a successful outcome for the coachee.

Adopting a non-directive approach and providing positive feedback

Another experienced coach intentionally adopts a non-directive approach, strengthening rapport by being positive and appreciative. She explains how her first steps in building rapport with the coachee involves taking three or four minutes to talk with her about her background. In terms of process, during the conversation she focuses on bringing the coachee's 'self-talk' to the fore as a way of helping the coachee challenge her own thinking and its effect on her own behaviour. She continuously plays back what the coachee is saying. She does this at several points throughout the conversation. Her coachee remarks how helpful she found it to hear her own words reflected back to her. The coachee reports that she found the continuous positive feedback very helpful. She also notes how that impacts on her relationship with the coach: 'It was reassuring and felt genuine ... Any confidence boost a person gets in a conversation is going to make the conversation flow more easily.' Interestingly, the coach notes the value of providing coachees with positive feedback during coaching and highlighted the potential for it to be perceived as insincere if it is not presented in a genuine and sensitive manner.

Using humour

An additional notable factor is the humour that a coach can bring to the coaching conversation. In one example, an experienced practitioner makes jokes, sometimes apparently at the coachee's expense, as an intentional challenge to her thinking. For example, the coach teases the coachee about her acceptance of positive feedback from others, with comments like 'and that's your manager just being nice' or 'and you said you're not very good at that?' These are challenges to the sense that the coachee, in reality, does not quite believe the positive statements she, and her manager, make about her performance. The coach brings up the American comedian Bob Newhart's counsellor sketch, where his response to his client's unhelpful behaviour is to continually tell her to simply 'Stop it!' Though light-hearted, there is a clear message that the coachee might do the same. There is laughter throughout the conversation, a feature that the coachee experiences as building the relationship with her coach. In reviewing his approach, the coach highlights his intention to demonstrate to the coachee that 'there is another human being here in the room'. For him, this playfulness feels like a natural response to the coachee's openness. However, he points out that there are sensitivities around a coach's use of humour that need to be taken into account.

See it in practice: Using own experience productively for the benefit of the coachee

Video 2.1

In this short clip, Denis recounts experiences that he had with other coachees (while protecting their anonymity) in order to normalise the coachee's dilemma. By doing this, he is building rapport with the coachee.

Above, we explored a number of factors associated with process and relationship in coaching. We considered how different coaches adopt various ways of establishing productive coaching relationships. One approach focuses on building the relationship before opening up the coachee's agenda for the session. The other hones in on the coachee's coaching topic quickly, using the process to strengthen rapport. Experienced practitioners will make decisions about how to work with the needs, interests and responses of individual coachees based on their circumstances and the context. What is clear is that each coach pays close attention to the relationship with the coachee. Sometimes experienced practitioners intentionally put the relationship front and centre, sometimes they make the coaching process paramount. For example, an experienced coach may challenge or use a coaching method that may be uncomfortable to the coachee. Causing a coachee to feel out of their comfort zone may put process and relationship into tension. Advanced practitioners make continual assessments about the quality of the relationship moment by moment and consider whether it is robust enough to underpin challenging processes.

THE PROFESSIONAL PERSPECTIVE

The Association for Coaching (AC) and the European Mentoring and Coaching Council (EMCC) 'Global Code of Ethics for Coaches, Mentors and Supervisors' provide guidance about how to start a coaching relationship, including the need to avoid creating coachee dependency (EMCC, 2018). A coach should establish relationships that are based on integrity, confidentiality and awareness of actual or potential conflicts of interest. Importantly, a coach is required to act in ways that recognise equality and diversity. The creation of safe environments and maintaining appropriate boundaries are seen as crucial for effective working relationships. In addition to establishing the foundation for a coaching relationship, the Code includes the importance of the relationships that exist beyond the coach and her coachee (i.e. with other stakeholders in the system). In terms of the coaching process, the Code establishes an expectation that a coach will keep herself up to date with developing coaching practices and will take part in regular supervision to review and extend her capabilities. It provides a foundation upon which to build the complex and intricate relationships that will enable productive work to be undertaken by the coach and her coachee.

In addition to the Global Code of Ethics, the competency frameworks devised by AC and EMCC both refer to the importance of establishing an effective coaching relationship. The AC emphasises a 'trust-based relationship' based on dignity, equality and respect, and the encouragement of the coachee's self-belief. A 'high level of rapport' is needed to build 'an open dialogue'. The coach should also accept the coachee 'as is' and believe in her 'potential and capability'. Maintaining confidentiality, acting 'openly and honestly', providing feedback and avoiding collusion are also factors in the AC framework.

One of the eight EMCC competence categories focuses on 'building the relationship'. The Council describes the 'senior practitioner capability indicators' in this area as involving:

- attending to and working 'flexibly with the client's emotions, moods, language, patterns, beliefs and physical expression'
- demonstrating 'a high level of attentiveness and responsiveness to the client in the moment while (being) mindful of the client's work towards outcomes'.

In addition, 'master practitioners' are able 'to describe their tactics in response to the client's sensory signals at every moment of a coaching conversation'.

The International Coaching Federation (ICF) has also established a set of 11 core coaching competencies, which include 'co-creating the relationship, based on "trust and intimacy" and "coaching presence"' (ICF, 2017). Clearly there is considerable overlap in the importance that the three professional associations place on the coaching relationship, with the EMCC providing a significant level of detail for coaches to use in evaluating their effectiveness at different levels of coaching capability.

PUTTING IT INTO PRACTICE

Patricia Bossons, Jeremy Kourdi and Denis Sartain outline a set of core principles that underpin all successful working relationships:

- displaying empathy and genuine warmth – being supportive, open, positive, constructive and engaging, not just being 'friendly'
- actively listening and questioning – to help build understanding and develop a genuine and informed bond
- being confident and self-aware – being challenging, in control, strong, authoritative, direct and understanding one's impact on others, own motivations and intentions
- displaying assertive behaviour – combining appropriate levels of support and challenge
- building trust by being diligent and consistent, acting with integrity and sincerity
- being considerate and realistic – understanding others' motivations, intentions and ways of working. (2012: 135)

These principles provide a baseline for considering how a coach needs to address the creation and maintenance of effective coaching relationships. Other writers build on these ideas by exploring the psychological aspects of the relationship.

For example, Alison Hardingham (2004) points to the importance of a coach meeting the coachee's basic psychological needs such as warmth, empathy, belonging and closeness. Van Nieuwerburgh extrapolates from research by Grencavage and Norcross into effective counselling relationships that coaches need to 'adopt a warm, attentive and positive approach' (2017: 16). Hardingham also suggests that the coach should pay attention to noticing the level of control the coachee wishes to exert in a session, which she acknowledges may change as the work progresses. The coach then engages in collaborative 'power sharing' with her coachee. Alongside awareness of the coachee's needs in relation to these psychological drivers, Hardingham underlines how vital it is for coaches to be acutely aware of their own needs and related behaviours in these areas.

Hardingham extends this discussion into the related 'danger points' that can arise in the coach–coachee relationship based on Douglas Stone, Bruce Patton and Sheila Heen's summary of the three essential questions, with which they suggest all human beings are preoccupied:

- Am I competent?
- Am I a good person?
- Am I worthy of love? (2000: 88)

According to Hardingham, threats to competence might arise from the coachee's perceptions of coaching, if her views or the organisational culture suggest that it is only poor performers who are 'sent' for coaching. Or the coach's questions may be interpreted as implying a negative judgement on the coachee's performance. Threats to 'goodness' or 'being confident that our contribution to others is positive' can occur if the coachee feels that her coach's assessment of her as a *person* is negative. Given the intimacy of a coaching relationship, such a perception can have profound effects. Threats to love can emerge for the coachee when she believes the coach does not 'accept', 'recognise' or 'value' her (Hardingham, 2004). Nancy Kline addresses the notion of love in 'thinking environments' (1999: 221). She emphasises the care involved in genuinely paying full attention to another person while at the same time 'holding on to yourself'. This is explored further in Chapter 8 (Being who you are and adapting to others).

Ioanna Iordanou, Rachel Hawley and Christiana Iordanou (2017: 51) review a recent research study (Machin, 2010) into the critical success factors in a coaching relationship, which underlines the importance of showing empathy, listening attentively, being non-judgemental and demonstrating congruence and acceptance. In addition, research into the coach–athlete relationship indicates that closeness (through trust and respect), commitment (developing a powerful and productive working partnership), complementarity (effective communication and clarity about roles) and co-orientation (based on open and honest communication) are key components (Jowett, Kanakoglou & Passmore,

2012). In this study both coaches and coachees singled out trust and honesty as crucial to a strong relationship (Iordanou, Hawley & Iordanou, 2017).

Throughout the discussion so far, we have seen that the coach should have high degrees of emotional intelligence in order to establish and sustain effective coaching relationships. Peter Hawkins and Nick Smith's relational engagement framework (2013: 277) helps coaches reflect on their abilities in four interrelated areas: capacity to connect to new worlds; capacity to process emotions; capacity to create a breadth of rapport; and capacity to develop depth of engagement. Anne Brockbank and Ian McGill's (2012) work reinforces the importance of the coach being able to work constructively with emotion, not least because it is the energy generated by feelings that is a key driver of double-loop learning. They also suggest that it is the relationship with another in a coaching arrangement that promotes transformational learning, beyond that which can be achieved through private, personal reflection alone (p. 53).

Based on the notion that every relationship develops a 'system dance', Mary Beth O'Neill (2007) suggests it is important for the coach to determine the types of dances she engages in with different coachees, to identify any patterns involved and consider whether those patterns assist or hinder coachees' development and coaching outcomes (p. 52). O'Neill is at pains to stress the systemic nature of these patterns believing that they illustrate vital factors about the system that the coach and coachee are co-creating, and they are also likely to reflect the coachee's relationship with the wider system (p. 65).

A seminal piece of work on the impact of one-to-one relationships has been undertaken by Erik de Haan (2008). By reviewing studies and carrying out new research into the effectiveness of one-to-one helping professions, de Haan isolates the common active ingredients as:

- the relationship – particularly all of its non-verbalised features, including the scheduling of solution-oriented sessions that focus on the coachee's situation
- the presence of the practitioner as a person, and their personality – coachees seem to be able to recognise the characteristics of a good practitioner
- the particular ideology to which the practitioner subscribes and bases her approach upon – it appears to be the practitioner's belief in and commitment to that ideology that is more influential than whether it has been shown to work.

De Haan (2008) describes the 'working alliance' (i.e. the quality of the partnership and relationship between coach and coachee) as one crucial factor affecting success. This working alliance is based on the client's 'affectionate relationship' with the practitioner, her motivation and ability to work collaboratively with the practitioner, the practitioner's empathic responses and involvement with the client, and agreement between the client and practitioner about the goals of the coaching. Given the lack of similar studies into the specifics of coaching, de Haan cautions about simply assuming that the results will transfer from the therapeutic setting into another field. However, he is confident enough of the potential similarities to propose some guidance (p. 48). See box below.

Focus on practice: Prioritising the relationship

Commit yourself heart and soul to your approach

While de Haan (2008) points out that the particular approach taken does not seem to be influential, it is the coach's *belief in and commitment to* a particular way of working that makes a difference, rather than the method itself.

Consider the coaching situation from your coachee's perspective

It seems that the coachee's expectations and perceptions of her coach are key. How the coachee experiences the 'working alliance' with her coach is central to a successful relationship.

Work on your coaching relationship

De Haan asserts that 'it is not just about the issue or the problem, and not even just about the coachees and their issues, or coachees and their organisations and *their* issues; it is actually mainly about the relationship' (p. 50). A strong relationship creates the conditions for more effective change.

If you don't 'click', find a replacement coach

Given the quality of the relationship is paramount, if the working alliance really is not working, de Haan suggests that starting a new relationship with a different coach is likely to produce better outcomes.

For de Haan, successful coaching is predominantly based on the quality of the relationship the coach is able to build with her coachee, who is the driver of her own change. De Haan defines relational coaching as 'active effort' by the coach to:

- understand how relationships impact the coachee's agenda – e.g. past and present relationships in her situation, and the relationship with the coach
- make the relationship as strong and productive as possible, 'as *experienced* by the coachee'

- use whatever specific interventions seem appropriate in the circumstances, bearing in mind the ideology adhered to by the coach and the over-arching intention to always work to strengthen the relationship
- maximise the common ingredients that have been shown to produce impact in other one-to-one helping arrangements. (2008: 53–4).

This thinking leads de Haan to conclude that the most effective coaching relationships comprise a series of 'critical moments', which increase opportunities for the coachee to 'self-understand' and 'self-change'. He sees critical moments as exciting, intense or significant moments, which occur in coaching conversations and are often associated with heightened emotions that cause, for example, exhilaration, curiosity, doubt or discomfort for the coachee, the coach or both. They can take many forms, from the coachee expressing something for the first time through to the seismic insights which turn things upside-down and lead to momentous changes in perception and action.

For de Haan these 'breakthrough' moments are a measure of the quality of the coaching relationship. While the coachee gains from the critical moments, so does her coach. They are a rich source of learning about practice for coaches, and becoming ready to notice and exploit these moments involves 'coaching with backbone and heart'. For example, 'in moments where fear of the new, uncertainty and doubt overcome coach and/or coachee, they are both closest to a breakthrough and to the possibility of real change through [the coaching relationship]' (2008: 57).

WIDER RELATIONSHIP CONSIDERATIONS

We have concentrated so far on the relationship between coach and coachee. As many writers acknowledge, particularly in the case of executive coaching, there are other relationships 'in the room'. The coach also has a relationship with other stakeholders in the coachee's organisation, including the sponsor of the coaching assignment, who is, in fact, the true client of the coach's services. In addition, in most organisational settings coaching conversations are very likely to include noticing and exploring the relationships the coachee has with significant others, such as colleagues she manages, peers and her own line manager. Taking a systemic perspective on these relationships, as advocated by, for example, Peter Hawkins and Nick Smith (2013), Mary Beth O'Neill (2007) and John Whittington (2016), therefore becomes a vital 'lens' for the coach to keep in mind. 'When you focus on the client alone ... you miss the whole grand ecosystem in which she functions. She is both influencing and being influenced by an entire web of inter-relationships in and around the organisation ... [and in] external contexts, which include the global economy and the natural environment' (O'Neill, 2007: 12). See Chapter 4 (Being fully present and attending to the wider context).

POWER IN COACHING RELATIONSHIPS

All human interactions have a power element built into them. Coaching is not immune to the impact of power on the relationship between coach and coachee. Little research has been undertaken into power dynamics in coaching, but a number of writers throw light on the paradox of how the coach uses her authority while at the same time relinquishing control to the coachee. Peter Hawkins and Nick Smith point to the influence of power differences in society, which can be mirrored, consciously and unconsciously, in the coaching relationship (2006: 305). Imbalances in power, related to a range of factors including gender, race, sexual orientation, disability, gender reassignment, class and status in the community and within organisations, can surface in the coaching conversation. Indeed, the coach, coming from her own particular cultural milieu, will import values, attitudes, behaviour and perspectives into the coaching relationship. The extent to which these aspects overlap with those of her coachee will vary to greater or lesser degrees depending on the differences between the two individuals involved. Some of these differences will be very obvious (i.e. race and gender) and will have a range of overt and covert implications. Other differences may appear minor, and yet will have great significance for the relationship. The experiences individuals have of the impact of their 'difference' will shape their interactions with the world, how confident and competent they have been made to feel and their expectations of the treatment they perceive they will receive from people from other backgrounds. Importantly, coach and coachee *assumptions* about their similarities and differences, whether accurate, entirely misplaced or somewhere in between, will also shape perceptions of each other, with knock-on effects on their relationship.

David Clutterbuck emphasises the importance in coaching of maximising the potentials of similarity and difference (2007: 141). He points out that high degrees of similarity between people in terms, say, of their identity and experience create the conditions for strong rapport to be established. The downside is that similarity can lead to 'group think' taking hold and the assumptions held in common going unchallenged. Where people's identities and experiences are very different there is high potential for learning because they have diverse perspectives to offer each other. Conversely, as a result of those differences, it may be more difficult, or take longer, to build a strong relationship. Advanced coaching practice embraces and works with these tensions in order to create strong, productive relationships that become the catalyst for learning.

Focusing on supervision, Peter Hawkins and Nick Smith suggest there are three distinct sources of power in play in the supervisor–coach relationship: role power, cultural power and personal power (2006: 305). The first embodies concepts of legitimate power, as derived from the position of supervisor. Cultural power is drawn from the social and cultural groupings people inhabit, the greatest power (at least in the western world) being located with white, middle class, heterosexual, able-bodied men. Personal power is grounded in, for example, the authority of a person's expertise, their presence and impact in the world, and their personality. For example, referent power is located here and involves the extent to which the supervisee wants to be like her supervisor. While the supervisor–coach relationship has its differences to that between coach and coachee, particularly in relation to the authority invested in the supervisor compared to the coach, it would be naive to suggest that the same aspects of power are absent when a coach meets a coachee.

In addition to socio-political factors, there are interpersonal, psychological forces in play. For example, coach and coachee may succumb to power games or become involved in acting out the three roles in a drama triangle (Karpman, 2014). Patricia Bossons, Jeremy Kourdi and Denis Sartain suggest that such power plays might be in pursuit of control and security by one person over the other (2012: 177). They point out that power plays might seem an easier route to take than to make the effort required to build the trust that will create a working relationship that is 'more durable, flexible and less brittle than [one based on] power' (p. 177). The building of trust, then, becomes an important means by which to avoid the power traps.

Much of the writing about power in the coaching relationship focuses on the different levels of authority the coach and coachee have at the beginning of the assignment, with a recognition that once the coaching progresses, the power balance shifts towards the coachee. Ioanna Iordanou, Rachel Hawley and Christiana Iordanou suggest that many relationships will start out unbalanced in this respect because at the beginning many coachees' understanding of coaching is incomplete or limited (2017: 57). This places the coach firmly in control in the initial phases of the coaching contract. Iordanou and her colleagues point out that this is unproblematic if the coach uses this knowledge power ethically and in the best interests of the coachee.

Acknowledgement that the coaching relationship *is* a relationship seems crucial to learning. Anne Brockbank and Ian McGill (2012) suggest that it is the quality of the coaching relationship that enhances or hinders insight and learning. Where the relationship is not concretely recognised as such there is 'a tendency for knowledge to be treated as static and disembodied, as a product rather than a process [and] coaches may treat their clients as detached, disembodied and passive ... inhibiting learning for the client' (p. 30). Julie Hay proposes that the most productive coaching relationships are 'development alliances' that 'depend on genuine connection, which 'will not work properly unless those involved believe that it is normal for people to want a close connection with each other' (quoted in Brockbank and McGill, 2012: 30).

So, the relationship in coaching is paramount, *and* process is important too. It is process that also makes a powerful contribution to distinguishing coaching from other kinds of conversations. Process forms an essential component of the structure that enables a session to be effective and marks coaching out as being a different quality of interaction. Advanced practitioners are adept at mobilising a range of coaching processes to meet the needs and interests of different coachees. They make on-the-spot decisions about what process, or adaptation of a process, might be helpful for the coachee in any particular moment. They have internalised a number of core approaches and deploy these with confidence and authenticity. While being highly responsive and flexible, they have faith that, in most circumstances, they can enable a process to produce outcomes for coachees. This self-belief is infectious and can help coachees, who may be reluctant to move outside their comfort zones, to suspend disbelief about a process and 'give it a go'. Advanced practitioners take calculated risks where necessary to stretch learning and growth, and crucially, encourage and support coachees to do the same. They are imaginative in their approach and tap into their own and others' creative energies to find new ways of seeing, thinking and doing. While they humbly recognise the limits of their understanding of the diverse breadth and depth of difference they encounter in working with coachees, they have a genuine interest in how diversity can be mobilised for the benefit of each coachee.

Early on in this chapter we talked about novice coaches' appetite for acquiring more and more coaching 'tools' as a route to becoming a better coach. Clearly, having a diverse portfolio of process possibilities is important. However, as we have suggested, a focus on the accumulation of techniques and methods may inadvertently risk becoming a hindrance to developing expertise in the creation and maintenance of coaching relationships. The reasonable desire to have another process 'up one's sleeve' in case the one being used doesn't quite work is understandable. The advanced practitioner is able to work with the 'failure' of process in the moment, rather than necessarily substitute a different model.

Perhaps the desire for more 'tools' over-emphasises the 'doing' element of coaching. Indeed, the term 'tool' with its mechanistic overtones may be an inaccurate piece of shorthand for the coaching process and encourages the belief that there is a 'right' approach *somewhere* in the 'toolkit'. Coaching, we believe, is one essential antidote to the downsides of our contemporary fast-paced, action-oriented work paradigm, which prioritises 'doing' over 'reflecting' and 'being'. With the pace of work life continuing to accelerate due to innovations in information technology (IT) and artificial intelligence (AI), the opportunities coaching provides to stand back and reflect on the busyness of everyday life will become even more valuable and necessary. In contrast, the pressures on coaches to race towards the solution part of the conversation are likely to increase. Writing on LinkedIn about mentoring, David Clutterbuck (2017) makes a powerful case for recognising that, though useful (and seductively cheap), 'fast knowledge transfer' through ad hoc, internet-enabled linkages between experts and solution-seekers has severe limitations, not least because the *relationship* element is missing. In addition, Ken Robinson (2001) has been engaged in a long-running and robust critique of contemporary education policy and methodologies for their failure to build young people's capacities to think for themselves and to use their creative faculties to the full. Coaching processes, which, through strong relationships, emphasise reflection, thorough analysis and thinking, emotional wellbeing and a holistic view of the coachee in her systemic setting will, in our view, become increasingly vital.

3
BEING CHALLENGING AND LETTING THINGS GO

Visit https://study.sagepub.com/advancedcoaching to watch the videos discussed in this chapter:

VIDEO 3.1: Confronting the coachee with his own contradictions
VIDEO 3.2: Providing challenging feedback
VIDEO 3.3: Making a decision to challenge rather than letting it go
VIDEO 3.4: Challenging the coachee to reflect more deeply

It is often argued that providing challenge is an important aspect of coaching (Blakey & Day, 2012; Rogers, 2016; van Nieuwerburgh, 2017). In our experience, coaching should be more than a 'comfortable conversation'. For coaching to be effective, there needs to be an appropriate balance of support and challenge. In this way, coaching can stretch a coachee's perception of the situation she faces, increasing her awareness and inviting her to see things differently. On this basis, a coach's reluctance to challenge could reduce the possibility of her coachee gaining transformational insights. Therefore, we propose that advanced practitioners should be prepared to challenge when it is in the best interest of their coachees. There will also be occasions when 'letting things go' will be a more powerful intervention. Advanced practitioners are able to hold both as possibilities (challenging and letting go) when coaching. How can coaches judge when to introduce a challenge? When might they withhold challenge because it feels more productive to do so? These questions are at the heart of this chapter.

To venture into this topic, it may be helpful to focus on what is meant by 'being challenging' in the context of a coaching conversation. In some cases, it might be an unobtrusive question that is not intended to be a challenge. For example, a coach might simply be summarising what she has heard. Sometimes, playing back what a coachee has said produces an unexpected pause in the conversation while the coachee considers and processes a new line of thinking. This kind of challenge can trigger an emotional response from the simple embodiment of surprised fascination through to a real shock that what had seemed so certain may now need serious re-evaluation. On the other hand, a coach may make an intentional and assertive intervention specifically designed to challenge the coachee. The deliberate intention is to shake up a coachee's thinking, inviting her to consider taking a dramatically different perspective or causing an immediate and serious pause for thought.

Stories from our practice: Using challenge to provoke new thinking

One of us recalls a coaching session he undertook with a senior public service manager, which began with the coachee dismissing other people's views of his performance as 'irrelevant'. Later in the conversation, in answer to the coach's question about how to test the success of a planned change in behaviour arising from the session, he replied: 'I'll ask other people.' The coach's follow-on question was 'and will you believe them this time?' The coachee slumped back in his chair and went quiet for a couple of minutes. Shining a light on the coachee's contradictory response triggered a deeper, more personal conversation about leadership style, which led to important insights for the coachee about his impact on colleagues.

Video 3.1

See it in practice: Confronting the coachee with his own contradictions

In this video, Denis uses an approach similar to the one described in the story above. He provides challenge by highlighting a contradiction that has emerged in the coachee's narrative.

Video 3.2

See it in practice: Providing challenging feedback

Helen's coaching session with her coachee is a conversation with motivation (for running) at its heart. Here Helen builds up the level of challenge gradually. Initially, she plays back the coachee's words by pointing out that 'Just listening to you, there's been a lot of "I could" or "I could try to" and so on ... it feels a little bit to me as if things are bouncing around'. Helen asks the coachee to expand on what is stopping her achieving her goal. The coachee's response is defensive and continues to range around different explanations for her inaction. Helen then presents a more confronting question: 'Would you describe yourself as a runner, now?' The coachee explains that she has not run seriously for a while and sees herself as an 'aspirational runner', which Helen acknowledges positively. This can be considered a 'critical moment' (de Haan, Bertie, Day & Sills, 2010). Helen's invitation to the coachee to reappraise her self-perception as a runner could be a negative turning point, reinforcing her lack of motivation to progress. Delivered at an inopportune moment, it could even undermine the coaching relationship. As a next step, Helen intentionally acknowledges the positive element of being an '*aspirational*' runner. She introduces the storyboarding technique as a way of exploring further. This is an *appreciative* process, which encourages and affirms the positive over the negative. Throughout the remainder of the session, Helen maintains a delicate balance of appreciative feedback (e.g. 'You *are* a successful runner') while stretching the coachee's thinking through progressive challenge.

See it in practice: Making a decision to challenge rather than letting it go

Video 3.3

In David's coaching session with the coachee, there are strong motivational elements to the coachee's goal for the session but there is a more pronounced negative overtone to the conversation. David decides to allow the coachee to stay with the negatives, 'sit with the discomfort' (van Nieuwerburgh, 2017) and explore these in more depth in the belief that their power is profound and will not be overcome by adopting a purely appreciative approach straight away. It is important that coachees feel listened to and understood. As she talks, David captures the main features of the coachee's situation on sticky notes so that these become visible and an overall picture can be built. At one point, David actively encourages a negative perspective when he expresses curiosity by asking the coachee 'Why did you come up with that as a positive?' Later, when reviewing the sticky notes, she even turns some previously positive features into negatives. The key challenges in this coaching conversation come in the second half, after the coachee has explored the realities of her current situation. Here David presses the coachee about her capacity and commitment to make a change in her behaviour. These challenges are signposted with statements and questions such as 'I'm going to push you a bit more', 'Can you do that?', 'How serious are you about changing things?' and 'What's it going to take to make some movement here?'

See it in practice: Challenging the coachee to reflect more deeply

Video 3.4

In this video, Bob presses the coachee to consider who she is trying to please. This evidently challenges the coachee and invites further reflection and discussion.

While we have highlighted examples of challenges in the videos above, there are also occasions when the coaches decided to let some challenges go. For example, Helen decides to take her coachee's description of herself as an 'aspirational runner' as a positive, whereas she might have chosen to underscore the negative undertones of that statement.

David could have challenged his coachee's perceived need for approval from him, which might have been another fruitful line of inquiry in which to take the conversation. In the moment, coaches make split-second decisions based on a diverse range of stimuli, including visual cues and the words being spoken. In Helen's case the intention was to tap into her coachee's feelings when she noticed her becoming more animated and engaged after expressing positive emotions about running. For David, while believing it to be important that his coachee worked through the negativity 'to come out the other side', he judged that introducing discussion of an apparent desire for approval into the conversation might have had a detrimental impact. Focusing on the relationship between coach and coachee might have broken the rapport, or even damaged that connection along with the potential for the eventual successful outcome.

When potential challenges are noticed but not pursued, the advanced practitioner does this for sound reasons. First, an advanced practitioner will be aware of the critical importance of the right relationship for productive coaching. For example, when the strength of the relationship is low and the degree of challenge is high, the chances of mistrust and the coachee becoming defensive are increased. On the other hand, if the strength of the relationship is high and the degree of challenge is low, there will be no drive for change and a risk of collusion by the coach. So advanced practitioners strive to maintain a balance between the strength of the relationship and the degree of challenge. In these circumstances, the coachee perceives the challenge as helpful though potentially uncomfortable, and new insights can arise (see Figure 3.1).

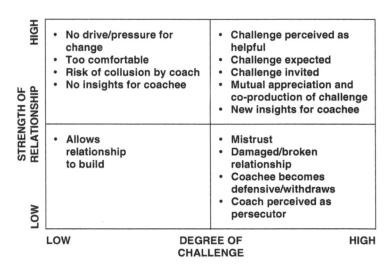

Figure 3.1 Relationship/challenge matrix

Second, a challenge might be passed over because the intervention could interrupt the coachee's flow and the advanced practitioner judges that interrupting her train of thought will not be helpful as she seems to be getting somewhere. She might just need more space, reflection, quietness and stillness to come to some insightful realisations for herself. Third, the advanced practitioner will often judge whether bringing additional topics into a coaching conversation might 'overload' the coachee for that session. In these instances, the challenge, especially if related to *patterns* of behaviour, might be held back for future conversations.

THE PROFESSIONAL PERSPECTIVE

Without challenge, there is unlikely to be sufficient stretch for coachees and less probability of new thinking or insights arising. Equally, the propensity for improved performance that has real impact on organisational achievements and outcomes for people in the wider system will be diminished. Given the importance of challenge, we should consider the thinking in the coaching field about this area of professional capability.

In its indicators of professional competence, the Association for Coaching (AC) makes three references to the use of challenge. It expects a coach to ask 'questions to challenge client's assumptions, elicit new insights, raise self-awareness and gain learning'. The AC also notes that a coach should explore 'what is working' and challenge 'lack of progress'. They use the phrase 'constructively challenge' in relation to the coach's role in supporting leaders to raise their standards (Association for Coaching, 2017). The European Mentoring and Coaching Council (EMCC) refers to coaches using 'feedback and challenge to help clients gain different perspectives, while maintaining rapport and responsibility for action' (European Mentoring and Coaching Council, 2017). For the EMCC, it is about the use of language to help coachees to 'reframe or challenge' their thinking or understanding. From the perspective of the International Coach Federation, there are three things that a coach should do: challenge a coachee's 'assumptions and perspective to provoke new ideas and find new possibilities for action'; provide challenge 'but also a comfortable pace of learning'; and 'positively confront' the coachee 'with the fact that he/she did not take agreed-upon actions' (International Coach Federation, 2017). While there are slight variations in explaining the intention of challenge in coaching conversations, there is broad agreement across the major professional associations about the need for coaches to be able to challenge their coachees.

RELEVANT THEORIES

Anne Brockbank and Ian McGill (2012) distinguish between different approaches to coaching and place *challenge* as a key element of successful coaching. They describe the limitations of 'functionalist coaching' that 'focuses on efficiency and equilibrium, assumes an objective real world, aims at improved performance and, in order to maintain the status quo, tends to suppress challenge and questioning' (p. 25). In response, they propose an 'evolutionary' approach to coaching, which 'acknowledges the subjective world of the client, respects ownership of the individual's goals and invites an examination of embedded power structures which inhibit learning' (p. 21). For these writers, openness to, and provision of, constructive and robust challenge is one of the ways to engage in such an examination. They place emphasis on the capacity of the coach to support the coachee with the disturbances caused by a challenge to the coachee's current assumptions, through working effectively with the 'emotional material flowing from such challenges' (p. 57), referencing the work of Gerard Egan. Author of *The Skilled Helper* (2013), Egan proposed three skills of challenging: advanced empathy, confrontation and immediacy. Advanced empathy involves the helper noticing or sensing indirectly (e.g. through non-verbal cues) emotional aspects that are not being expressed overtly by the client, and which she may not even be aware of herself. Egan emphasises the crucial importance of a strong relationship being required as a launchpad for challenge. This relationship, through continuous contracting and the strengthening of trust experienced as the connections mature, creates the conditions in which challenge can take place.

The word 'confrontation' may have negative connotations for some people. People's experiences of conflict and personality factors can influence how they perceive confrontation (Antonioni, 1998). In some cases, people view confrontation as a threat or a personal attack, rather than as a positive opportunity to question assumptions and develop new insights. John Heron proposes that 'constructive confrontation' involves telling 'the truth with love, without being the least judgmental, moralistic, oppressive or nagging' (1999: 182). For the advanced practitioner, this means not being attached 'to what you say, you can let it go as well as hold firmly and uncompromisingly to it' (p. 182). Brockbank and McGill (2012) underline that 'confronting here has nothing to do with the aggressive, combative' forms that are the norm in legal, political and industrial dispute scenarios. They also acknowledge that challenge can generate anxiety in the coach, who anticipates the potential difficulties of the coachee. Referring to Heron again, they describe two main options for presenting a challenge: 'pussyfooting, being so "nice" that the issue is avoided, or clobbering, being so punitive that' the impact is 'wounding'. 'The challenge', Heron asserts, 'is to get it right. Too much love and you collude. Too much power and you oppress. When you get it right, you are on the razor's edge between the two' (1999: 183).

Another insightful writer on this topic is Mary Beth O'Neill, who sees the role of the executive coach as a partner in the process of enabling her client to achieve business results within her organisational context. O'Neill invokes the concept of 'signature presence', by which she means the coach bringing her 'ideas, biases and ability to constructively challenge' (2007: 14) within strong relationships established with clients. She coins the phrase 'coaching with backbone and heart'. 'Backbone means knowing and clearly stating your position, whether it is popular or not. Heart is staying engaged in the relationship and reaching out even when that relationship is mired in conflict' (p. 14).

For O'Neill, bringing backbone to coaching conversations involves:

- the coachee knowing what the coach thinks, including the coach stating her agreement or disagreement with the coachee
- identifying what the coach needs from her coachee in the coaching relationship in order to be most effective
- the coach stating her position or opinion without blame, defensiveness or jargon
- giving 'hard feedback' when required.

In parallel, bringing heart means the coach:

- empathising with the coachee's situation
- clearly articulating the coachee's position and reflecting this back accurately
- identifying and communicating 'hunches' about 'deeper reactions, feelings, thoughts', which are left unexpressed
- staying 'in touch' with the coachee throughout the session
- expressing appreciation for the 'degree of difficulty in the client's situation' and for her achievements
- tuning into the relationship with understanding and compassion. (2007: 15)

Here we have a leading thinker in the field focusing on the possibility of conflict or tension in coaching conversations, a position which might seem contrary to a more traditional view of coaching as an inherently supportive, collaborative interaction. Implicit in O'Neill's approach is a more directive coaching stance, which accords with the authoritative interventions discussed by John Heron (1975). According to Heron, the three authoritative interventions include 'informing, prescribing and confronting'. An *informing* authoritative intervention would involve providing new information or knowledge to someone. Advising, offering an opinion, being critical, evaluating performance or otherwise seeking to direct a person's behaviour would be considered a *prescribing* authoritative intervention. A *confronting* authoritative intervention would mean that one person was challenging the restrictive attitudes, beliefs or behaviours of another.

Clare McGregor of the Coaching Inside and Out charity works with offenders in prisons. Through her compelling work, she demonstrates the importance of challenge by showing that it can impact on behaviour and generate new perceptions. She points to the importance of the coach 'holding up the mirror', but warns against this process simply becoming an 'echo chamber' where challenge is avoided. Listening with empathy is just the first step, 'the power of coaching lies in the tension you create for the client' (2015: 85). 'Silence and biting your tongue are two of the hardest things client and coach have to deal with' (p. 85). McGregor describes how she and her fellow coaches need to 'let go of things' by learning not to interrupt the coachee's thought processes. According to McGregor, 'interruptions should be to open up new avenues to learn about the client, not the situation' (p. 85). This is an insightful and practically impactful distinction for advanced practitioners to consider.

Other writers in the field encourage coaches to take a more directive, confronting approach in challenging coachees. John Blakey and Ian Day in their book *Challenging Coaching* (2012) assert that most coaching is skewed towards support for the individual, rather than provocative challenge that would have positive impact in the system. They argue that challenge should be delivered from the basis of a relationship of trust and respect. While Blakey and Day acknowledge the importance of rapport in the therapeutic setting, they question the centrality of continuous, strong rapport to the effectiveness of coaching. According to Blakey and Day, helping a coachee to focus on matters that affect her performance will require robust challenge which, by its nature, is likely to temporarily disrupt rapport.

Somatic coach Eunice Aquilina approaches the seeming paradox of challenging and letting go from a different angle. She suggests that our societies teach us to avoid conflict but asserts that we are missing an important opportunity for greater self-awareness if we do not 'learn to swim in the waters of conflict, going beyond seeing conflict as something where there is a winner and a loser' (2016: 107). Aquilina believes that we need to see conflict as a 'generative space, an opportunity for something new and different to be born or a time to innovate and create anew' (p. 107). She sees conflict-avoidance as arising from people's conditioning 'driven by their fundamental need for safety and belonging' (p. 108). This suggests that advanced practitioners need to move away from any assumptions and projections about the coachee and develop a curiosity about what might be occurring 'in the moment'. This will involve advanced practitioners 'surrendering to the uncertainty and stepping into [their] vulnerability' (p. 108). For Aquilina, 'surrender' does not mean giving in but 'letting go of those automatic responses that serve to defend us so well but that limit' our effectiveness (p. 108). She recognises the difficulties and discomforts of taking this position for both coach and coachee. Those moments when advanced practitioners are shining a light on something that coachees might prefer to keep out of sight can place us in potential conflict and threaten coaching relationships. However, this is where advanced practitioners 'can really add value, helping people see beyond their habitual perspective on the world, deepening their awareness so they can exert more choice for themselves in how they want to show up in their work and in their life' (p. 111). In this sense, advanced practitioners need to be prepared to challenge *themselves* to work effectively with discomfort and let go of their fear of conflict in the best interests of coachees.

It is generally accepted that good practice in coaching involves the coach offering an appropriate degree of constructive challenge, balanced with support. A coaching conversation with no challenge at all is likely to miss important opportunities for the coachee to test her assumptions, thinking and ideas about the future. Advanced practice involves being thoughtful about the way challenge is presented to the coachee, with an emphasis on 'elegance' and with intention and outcome firmly focused on the benefits for the coachee, her stakeholders and her sponsor. Essentially, effective challenge involves 'holding up a mirror' for the coachee to see herself more clearly and make judgements about the accuracy and appropriateness of her assumptions, thinking and emotions. Even when it is uncomfortable to do so, the advanced practitioner will provide challenge if it might help the coachee to achieve her goals or overcome barriers. Equally, the advanced practitioner will make considered decisions about when certain topics or issues should be allowed to slide into the background. In both cases, the decision to challenge or to let go should be made with the best interests of the coachee in mind.

Based on our exploration in this chapter, advanced practitioners should be able to make informed decisions about what and when to challenge, when to let something go and when to return to a topic they have implicitly or explicitly set to one side. They make subtle judgements, based on a range of cues beyond the coachee's words, about the timing and presentation of a challenging intervention. In addition to challenging assumptions and thinking, they can challenge the emotional content of a coaching conversation with awareness that feelings may be more important than thoughts, and that too often traditional coaching can tend to focus on the cognitive rather than the affective and creative.

Focus on practice: Deciding when to challenge or let things go

Assess the strength of the relationship

It is helpful to pay attention to the relationship with the coachee. Advanced practitioners assess whether the relationship is in a condition to remain productive in the light of a challenge that might threaten to undermine or disrupt the rapport that has been established. If a relationship is broken, it can endanger the agreed purpose of the coaching contract. This highlights the critical importance of the contract agreed with the coachee at the outset of a series of coaching sessions and at the beginning of each conversation. Advanced practitioners include an exploration about the level of challenge sought by the coachee. With this foundation in place, it becomes easier for the advanced practitioner to offer, and the coachee to receive, challenging feedback or questions. In addition, being cognisant of the need for continuous contracting throughout the coaching relationship allows for

(Continued)

(Continued)

individual instances of challenge to be accommodated. This suggests that advanced practice involves a high degree of overt or subtle negotiation as to the direction, pace and tone of the conversation.

Adopting a stance of 'fearless compassion'

The concept of 'fearless compassion' (Hawkins and Smith, 2013: 274) relates to the extent to which a coach is prepared to 'speak the truth', or encourage the truth to be spoken. This takes place within a framework that is caring and holds the coachee in a safe place to take advantage of the opportunity for new insights. Advanced practitioners use challenge elegantly, finding ways to present challenge in a constructive, purposeful and engaging way. 'Elegant challenge' (Thompson, 2017) can be understood as the ability to:

- be tactful and constructive (ensuring that the challenge is not perceived as a personal attack)
- avoid 'cornering' the coachee, and allowing them to acknowledge a difficulty without being humiliated
- pay attention to time and context (a carefully chosen moment can make a big difference)
- avoid being punitive, given the aim is to help the coachee to learn and develop, not to create unnecessary friction
- take account, explicitly or implicitly, of the potential vulnerability of the coachee in the moment
- present the challenge in a genuine spirit of compassion and a commitment to the coachee gaining insights and learning.

Making 'in-the-moment' decisions

Advanced practitioners make rapid, on-the-spot decisions about what to challenge or let go. They base their decisions on the quality of the relationship with the coachee, the agreed purpose of the coaching and a broader sense of what might be helpful to the coachee in her organisational and systemic context (see Chapter 4: Being fully present and attending to the wider context).

Making 'in-the-moment' decisions about challenging or letting go requires coaches to:

- find ways of being fully present in the coaching session
- notice moments when challenge or letting go may be appropriate
- continually be aware of the strength of the coaching relationship

- show acute sensitivity to the coachee's personalised perspective which blends a diverse array of factors such as, for example, class, race, gender and professional background
- assess the vulnerability of the coachee in the moment
- be courageous (demonstrating fearless compassion) if challenge is required
- be graceful (elegant) if it is appropriate to let something go.

4
BEING FULLY PRESENT AND ATTENDING TO THE WIDER CONTEXT

Visit https://study.sagepub.com/advancedcoaching to watch the video discussed in this chapter:

VIDEO 4.1: Encouraging the coachee to acknowledge the wider context

In order to build the robust professional relationships discussed in Chapter 2 (Being focused on process and prioritising the relationship), advanced practitioners develop ways to be fully present when they are with their coachees. It is this 'presence' that we will discuss in this chapter. While there is little doubt that the ability to be present and 'in the moment' is necessary for coaches, we should note that this may bring with it the risk of becoming excessively invested in the coachee as an individual, rather than staying alert to the broader, strategic context in which she operates. Ideally, advanced practitioners should be able to be fully present while also remaining conscious of the systemic context and aware of its potential implications.

Focus on practice: Being fully present

An experienced coach starts a coaching conversation with the phrase 'so here we are'. This seems a prescient way to open a coaching conversation. He remarks on the reality of the presence of two people in the room, signalling at the same time the need for both to be present *in the moment*. This need for both coach and coachee to be 'in the room' (not just in the physical sense) is essential for meaningful conversations to take place. Throughout the session, the coach presents a steady and calm demeanour, fully in the moment with the coachee. His body language, facial expressions and gestures indicate attentiveness and

(Continued)

(Continued)

interested connection with the coachee. At the start of the conversation, the coach provides a reflective space in which the coachee could open up and begin to explore her topic. The coach's calm energy is a silent yet powerful invitation to the coachee. Through his non-verbal behaviours, the coach says 'this conversation is about you'. The coachee points out that the topic is one she had thought about before without reaching a satisfactory conclusion. This is a regular occurrence in coaching. Often, people who have spent a considerable amount of time perusing an important matter are not able to find a desirable way forward. After the session, the coach expresses his curiosity about why the unfolding topic was an issue at all for the coachee. On the surface, it seems a straightforward case of allocating the time to make something happen. The coach set aside the opportunity to form a judgement allowing his curiosity to maintain his presence and engagement, confident in the belief that the coachee would reveal to herself the reason for the importance of the issue.

Video 4.1

See it in practice: Encouraging the coachee to acknowledge the wider context

In this video, Christian asks the coachee to imagine that she was asked to give advice to a new employee in order to raise the coachee's awareness of the professional and cultural context in which she works.

PERSPECTIVES ON PRESENCE

The concept of presence is often discussed in coaching communities. Most experienced coaches would agree that being fully present is essential during coaching. According to the International Coach Federation (ICF), presence is 'the ability to be fully conscious and create a spontaneous relationship with the client, employing a style which is open, flexible and confident' (ICF, 2017). Because of the importance of developing powerful relationships, advanced practitioners are fully present in their coaching conversations. According to Paul Brown and Denyse Busby-Earle (2014), being 'fully present' requires coaches to be highly aware of their own emotions, the emotions of their coachees, and the interplay between these. From this perspective, it is important that coaches listen 'with and for emotions' (p. 137). For Patsy Rodenburg (2009), one of the leading experts on presence in the theatre, it is all about energy and the way it flows. First, at its essence there is the energy of survival. Rodenburg argues that a lack of presence can put people in danger because they become unaware of the risks around them. She points out that sometimes we notice presence by its absence. For example, the actor who does not communicate presence will be overlooked by the audience in favour of the person on stage who does. From this unique perspective, Rodenburg explores how presence can be *lost*. As many advanced practitioners will appreciate, modern life presents multiple barriers to being present. For Rodenburg, presence is related to intimacy: 'Two human beings present together experience intimacy and knowledge of one another, and each person understands something of the other's story and, consequently, their humanity' (p. 4). Clearly this has important implications for coaches. As we have already discussed, the quality of the relationship is a key factor that can be influenced by advanced practitioners (see Chapter 2: Being focused on process and prioritising the relationship). Intimacy in coaching relationships will be discussed later in this chapter.

Drawing on Zen Buddhism, Eckhart Tolle (2011) acknowledges that *thinking* about presence is problematic. According to him, we can only truly understand what presence is when we are *actually present* rather than thinking about being present. This is an important consideration for coaches. What matters most for coachees is their *experience* during the coaching conversation. While there is increasing academic study and research into the effectiveness of coaching (Theeboom, Beersma & van Vianen, 2014), we must recognise that it is an *applied* discipline. Theories and processes can only be helpful to practitioners if they have a positive impact on the experience of coaching clients.

From a Buddhist perspective, a prerequisite of presence is to be deeply rooted in oneself. The implication for advanced practitioners is that they should be aware of their energy levels and conscious of what their bodies are doing, even more than reflecting on the need to be present. According to this point of view, it is through experiencing being present that coaches can more regularly be in the moment with their coachees. In his book, *Presence-based Coaching* (2008), Doug Silsbee moves beyond understanding presence as a set of behaviours utilised to achieve a purpose. Elaine Patterson takes this idea further: 'Presence is an alive and freeing state of generous, compassionate and mindful awareness in our being – which is felt and experienced – in the here and now in the relationship with another; and which opens our hearts, minds and bodies to a wider reality and joyful field of connectedness, possibility and potential' (2011: 117–37). For MacKenzie (2013), presence is not only about impact, it is about building and sustaining the conditions for insights to emerge. While recognising that it is important to behave in certain ways with others in order to demonstrate presence, Silsbee argues that being present incorporates the elements of behaviour and way of being. Mary Beth O'Neill (2007) beautifully captures this requirement by coining the term 'coaching with backbone and heart'. In her view, presence is characterised by the development and maintenance of the coach's tolerance for 'ambiguity, daunting challenges, the anxiety or disapproval of others, and [our] own personal sources of stress' (p. 20). This allows advanced practitioners to face challenging situations head on (with 'backbone') in order to use them to support coachees to gain valuable insights.

We can also approach presence from a slightly different angle. Shiatsu therapist training sees the presence of the practitioner as vital to the success of treatments. Ryokyu Endo describes the relationship between the giver and receiver of shiatsu thus: 'The union between the healer and the patient is not the joining of the two into one but the loss of boundaries as each comes into contact with the other and both enter a state of nothingness. When the boundaries between ourselves and others are lost, we may feel infinite nothingness without perception of space and time – and feel life as one source: here and now' (1995: 78). It is worth noting the similarities with the positive psychology concept of 'flow' (Csikszentmihalyi, 2002). Coaches may struggle with the idea that a goal of relationships is 'nothingness'. Yet historically, Eastern healing traditions see this as a state from which the therapist can begin to provide benefit through tuning in and noticing what is happening in the patient's body. Given our discussion in this chapter about the vital importance of presence, perhaps this 'nothingness', elusive though it is, might be where coaches can find a foundation from which to open up and identify creative ways to support their coachees.

Endo goes on to state that 'a close connection with others should be fundamental to all human relations. However, modern times have brought about a disintegration into illness. Recently, sympathy and contact between people have weakened, and as we become more self-centred, our main concerns are individualism and isolationism. Our relationship with nature has also weakened, and we have lost focus on our bodies, our closest connection with nature' (1995: 78). This view suggests that we should be cautious about relying too heavily on cognitive approaches. Advanced practitioners need to fine tune the balance between thinking about ways forward and being in the moment.

PRESENCE AND MINDFULNESS

Liz Hall (2013) explores the relationship between mindfulness and presence. She contends that mindfulness is the means through which it is possible for a coach to achieve presence. Hall understands presence as a state of being open and unattached to a particular course of action or outcome. Dan Siegel (2010) supports this view by proposing that presence requires an openness to whatever happens in reality. This requires a tolerance for uncertainty and ambiguity. Presence, according to Hall, incorporates some of the following elements:

- listening deeply
- being open to possibility
- being available
- being warm
- being vulnerable
- a feeling of connectedness and interconnectedness. (2013: 45)

LISTENING TO UNDERSTAND

Coach training programmes focus heavily on the skill of listening. The quality of listening needed during coaching conversations is different from the type of listening required for everyday interactions. Coaches listen to understand more often than listening for information. In our experience of working with trainee coaches, there is a dramatic shift in the quality of listening as the power of *being listened to* is experienced – and this shift can take place quite early during a training programme. Novice coaches soon notice that high-quality listening is one of the ways of building a strong connection with coachees. We would argue that this realisation is a key development stage for all coaches. Of course, because novice coaches are still learning, this realisation (of the value of listening to understand deeply) is coupled with concerns and anxieties about 'doing it right'. And many novice coaches are also battling against a tendency to provide solutions or make suggestions. So while they grow to recognise the critical importance of listening to understand deeply, they are also trying to be fully present and fully focused. They are also unlearning conversational habits such as filling silences or overly focusing on what they will say next while the coachee is still speaking. As a result, the quality of listening (demonstrated in the ability of the coach to be fully present) develops over time as the coach becomes more experienced and grows in confidence.

THE HUMAN ELEMENT

Hall refers to 'being open to possibility' and 'being available' as elements of presence. Again, these can only emerge out of experience. Novice coaches must move beyond conscious incompetence – at the start of an introductory training programme; to conscious competence – during the early stages of learning to be a coach; and finally to unconscious competence – through experience and reflective practice. Only when coaches feel relatively comfortable about their ability to coach can they be 'open to possibility' and 'available' during coaching conversations. Not having to worry about 'am I doing it right?' or being distracted by self-doubt permits coaches to be less guarded, allowing them to be more authentic. To use Hall's words, coaches can be 'warm' (and personable) while also showing 'vulnerability'. Coaches are then able to connect with their clients at a very human level. In essence, coach and coachee connect through their shared humanity. This is often different from our everyday professional interactions which can be stylised and formalised. Confusingly, the experience can be more akin to intimate personal relationships with loved ones. Advanced practitioners need to manage this carefully. Coaching relationships should be strong and intimate in the sense that they are personal, private and confidential. It is important that coachees feel that their coaches genuinely care about their success and wellbeing (see Chapter 9: Being committed to outcomes and prioritising wellbeing). However, advanced practitioners recognise that coaching relationships are *professional* relationships that are built specifically for the purpose of supporting their coachees to learn and develop in meaningful ways. As a result, advanced practitioners think carefully about boundaries. While advanced practitioners may be friendly, they make it clear that they are not there to become friends with their coachees. Advanced practitioners are skilled at starting and ending coaching relationships. They tend to have clear and consistent processes that are applied to each of their clients. Managing boundaries in order to have impactful coaching relationships is essential for the wellbeing of coaches and coachees while also protecting the good name of coaching as a profession.

THE GESTALT APPROACH: HERE AND NOW

Gestalt has a rich history in the field of psychotherapy and has recently been applied to coaching (Leary-Joyce, 2014). As an approach, it encompasses a broad range of theoretical concepts that help to keep attention on the 'here-and-now' rather than perceptions and thoughts based on past experience. It is often said that the German word *gestalt* is difficult to translate to English but is commonly understood as 'the whole' (particularly in the sense of the following quote that is attributed to Aristotle: 'The whole is greater than the sum of the parts'). The Gestalt approach understands the human being as a 'whole entity' comprising body, mind and soul. Its focus is to increase self-awareness so that clients can understand themselves better. From a Gestalt perspective, coachees are encouraged to experience and reflect on the relationship between a person's thinking, behaviour and choices. The 'here-and-now' aspect of the Gestalt approach is relevant to our discussion of being present.

According to Gestalt concepts, it is in the here-and-now that awareness can be best explored: 'It is within the here and now that current awareness arises, and contact, growth and change emerge' (Spoth, Toman, Leichtman & Allan, 2016: 388). Gestalt coaches carry out 'experiments' or 'interventions' in the here and now as a way of offering the client increased awareness and understanding. These experiments are co-created with the coachee, 'derived from the here and now work of the session, and emerge from the client's field of experience' (pp. 388–9). The coach and coachee are able to discuss the insights and awareness that may have emerged through experimentation in the moment during the session. In fact, Gestalt practitioners would argue that 'the only place where growth is possible is the ever present here and now' (p. 394).

In some ways, the Gestalt approach challenges the principles and practices taught in introductory coach training programmes. To present the case simply, it could be argued that such coach training programmes suggest that coaching sessions are facilitated conversations that are centred on thinking about possible changes to behaviour. According to this perspective, the change in behaviour takes place in between coaching conversations. That means that the coaching sessions are considered to be primarily theoretical, with the coachee required to experiment with her new ideas and strategies in the real world before reconvening to analyse and discuss what was learned through the experimentation. This creates the sense that the coaching conversations take place somewhere other than the real world. This 'non-real world' space is then understood as a place of safety and reflection that is somehow separate from the realities that the coachee wishes to discuss. Gestalt coaches believe that change happens in the moment, and therefore it is taking place during the coaching conversation. And it is this belief that leads Gestalt practitioners to argue that coaches must be fully present in the moment in order to work with whatever is happening in the session while also being open to whatever might emerge. Learning and change take place all the time, including during the coaching conversation itself.

THE WIDER CONTEXT: THINKING SYSTEMICALLY

As if the seeming contradiction between what is taught in introductory coaching courses and the Gestalt approach were not complicated enough, we propose that advanced practitioners find ways to be fully in the moment during coaching conversations whilst also being conscious and alert to systemic factors that have an impact on their coachees. We believe that advanced practitioners should demonstrate their presence during the coaching conversation in order to build strong and meaningful relationships with their coachees. At the same time, we recognise that advanced practitioners will want to maintain sufficient professional detachment so that they are able to bring a different perspective to the conversation and raise their coachees' full understanding of their objectives and desires within their personal and professional contexts.

The term 'systemic coaching' has attracted much interest, particularly within professional contexts (Whittington, 2016). The underpinning idea is that systemic coaching incorporates the complexity that surrounds the coachee and her intentions. Its aim is to support professionals to work effectively within their environments by raising awareness about, and working with, what is going on around them. Coachees are invited to pursue personal success by reflecting on what motivates them, considering ways of improving key relationships and being aware of the professional environments in which they operate. Whittington is one of the leading figures in the field of systemic coaching. When delivering training on the approach he asks participants to 'imagine all the systems in which your client has belonged, behind them, like a peacock's tail'. The systemic approach recognises that coaches and coachees each operate within larger systems. It acknowledges that human beings are interconnected. Whittington argues that the extent of this interconnectedness is often overlooked or goes unnoticed in other coaching approaches. In executive coaching, this interconnectedness becomes critically important because leaders and managers need to work effectively *within* their professional contexts and collaboratively with other stakeholders to be successful. While it is sometimes assumed that systemic coaching focuses on the client and her environment, there are other layers of complexity that an advanced practitioner keeps in mind. For example, not only do advanced practitioners recognise the systemic context of their clients, they are also aware of their own systemic context. Both the client's system and the coach's system will have effects on the coaching conversation.

Jennifer Plaister-Ten adopts a systemic approach that focuses on the important, and often subtle, impacts of culture. She describes the main features of culture as relating to family, nation, gender, religion, ethnicity, generation, region, community and organisation and emphasises the nuanced ways in which such factors are interpreted by, and combine, to shape each individual's behaviour, thinking and emotions in an increasingly multicultural world. 'Potentially, we no longer live in a world of either/or, but of both/and: a world where paradox is normal and where knowledge is emergent'. Working with coachees from diverse backgrounds 'will necessitate [coaches] having to know ourselves – our cultural values – in order to be able to identify what to carry forward and what to leave behind'. Coaches 'can facilitate this by asking the incisive questions necessary to identify not only cross-cultural but cross-functional patterns and to cut through complexity' (2016: 12).

A systemic approach requires the coach to be conscious that there will be a range of contextual factors and influences that will inform and impede or support the coachee to achieve her and her organisation's aspirations or goals. The advanced practitioner invites the coachee to see things from other perspectives or through different lenses so that she becomes more aware of the interconnections. In doing so, systemic coaching aims to increase alignment between the coachee and her context.

BEING PRESENT WHILE MAINTAINING PROFESSIONAL DETACHMENT

It would seem that being present is an essential prerequisite for a successful coaching conversation because it ensures that the coachee can be fully heard, valued and appreciated. To deliver this level of presence, advanced practitioners develop strategies to be mindful and calm. They bring serenity to the coaching relationship. This serenity allows an advanced practitioner to be alert to what is happening during the coaching conversation, increasing the chances that she will be open to whatever emerges. In this way, coachees have the opportunity to experiment, learn and grow during the coaching conversation itself, allowing for exploration, creativity and discovery.

Focus on practice: What advanced practitioners do to be fully present while attending to the wider context

- Allow coachees to trust in the process of the conversation by creating the conditions for them to open up about their topics.
- Hold a curious stance as a means of staying focused on helping coachees work things out.
- Find ways to maintain a strong connection with coachees.
- Remain alert to coachees' emotions while monitoring and managing their own feelings.
- Remain aware of indicators that they are getting too drawn into their coachees' worlds.
- Be conscious of personal preferences in relation to complexity and ambiguity.
- Reflect on what is happening for them prior to each coaching conversation.

It is more likely that coachees will be fully present and engrossed in the session if the coach demonstrates that she is fully present too. While not ignoring the cognitive and behavioural aspects of coaching, simply *being* is an important part of building effective relationships. This is the seeming paradox: the advanced practitioner is *in* the session whilst also figuratively stepping out of the conversation in order to retain a wider perspective. Every advanced practitioner will learn to manage this in her own way.

5

BEING TENACIOUS AND ENCOURAGING AUTONOMY

Visit https://study.sagepub.com/advancedcoaching to watch the video discussed in this chapter:

VIDEO 5.1: Encouraging the coachee to have a conversation with herself

See it in practice: Encouraging the coachee to have a conversation with herself

Video 5.1

In this coaching conversation, Helen starts by helping her coachee to identify the factors that keep her from taking up running again. From the early stages of the session, Helen encourages her coachee to recognise that she has control over her behaviour and helps her to focus on the motivational factors that are in play. Through the process, the coachee identifies practical actions that will help her strengthen her motivation to behave differently and break the impasse that keeps her from creating a new habit. This helps her to reconnect with her strong desire to run, both for her health and fitness, and as a social activity with friends and colleagues. Identifying these practical steps builds the coachee's commitment to change. In the video clip, Helen builds a sense of autonomy in the coachee by asking her to 'have a conversation with herself'.

Coaches enable their coachees to be autonomous and make informed decisions that improve their performance and impact. Autonomy is at the heart of what coaches do. So, what is this concept, how does it play out in the lives of coachees and how can advanced practitioners remain constructively persistent in enabling people to embrace significant personal change?

PERSPECTIVES ON AUTONOMY

A principle underpinning coaching is that a coach believes her coachee is an autonomous individual who, with time, reflection and encouragement, can craft a way of taking forward the challenge or success she has brought to the coaching session. Gillon (1985) defines autonomy as relating to a person's independent right to decide her own course of action without any external pressure or influence.

For the Association for Professional Executive Coaching and Supervision (APECS), autonomy is a foundational ethical principle underpinning all coaching activity. According to APECS principles, coaches will 'help individuals and companies make their own decisions and move towards increasing self-authority' (apecs.org; accessed 13 December 2018). This echoes the view of psychotherapists for whom 'promoting the autonomy of those one provides services to, is one of [the] over-arching goals. This includes respect for the client's right and ability to be self-governing' (de Jong, 2010: 208). Autonomy also forms a vital component in human relationships. Ilona Boniwell, citing Peterson and Seligman (2004), proposes that 'autonomous adults find it quite easy to get close to others, are trusting and trustworthy, and are comfortable with mutual co-dependence' (2012: 121). This view has significant benefits for building the effective relationships that are essential to coaching success. In Gestalt thinking, the need for personal autonomy is seen in balance with the need for affiliation with others. Edwin Nevis applies this interconnection to the workplace and writes about individuals 'going it alone' versus 'going it married' (2001: 190). In relation to the former, the individual has 'a strong desire to control her way of working and have minimum requirements to make adjustments for the wishes or preferences of others' (p. 190). Conversely, the drive for affiliation involves 'a strong desire for belonging, coordinated effort, and ... awareness that some degree of personal submission may be advantageous and thus worth accepting' (p. 190). Professionals in the workplace are constantly making cost–benefit analyses about the degrees of autonomy and affiliation that will suit their preferences, style and circumstances.

Self-determination theory (SDT) highlights the importance for wellbeing of the connections between autonomy (having a sense of choice) and affiliation, here referred to as 'relatedness' (being in community with others) along with a third key factor, competence (using capabilities to make an impact) (Ryan & Deci, 2000: 70). Ryan and Deci suggest that autonomous motivation is developed through leadership behaviours that include, for example, asking open questions, active listening, offering choices and providing feedback, in other words the core elements of effective coaching. They also suggest that coaching can help a coachee to convert extrinsic motivation (doing things for externally controlled reasons) to intrinsic or autonomous motivation (doing things for more freely chosen reasons) through opportunities to see how 'imposed' goals might be integrated with desired outcomes. In this way, greater levels of ownership, autonomy and sustainable commitment are generated. This can result in higher levels of wellbeing and performance.

In addition to autonomy being an essential ingredient for wellbeing, it has important implications for workplace effectiveness and performance. Focusing on the benefits of diversity in business, Binna Kandola writes: 'The degree of autonomy felt by people in an organisation will have a bearing on their readiness to [see things from different perspectives]. Where people feel that they are component parts of a machine designed and run by someone else, they are absolved from caring about the other people implicated in their actions. One way of thinking about the diversity movement is to see it as a powerful expression of our need to rehumanise work, after a long period of industrialisation. Society has gone as far as it can with mechanisation … That's why people at work need autonomy: without it, the organisation will atrophy' (2009: 193). Doug MacKie (2016) argues that toxic organisational cultures are usually characterised by a lack of autonomy for employees. For toxicity to prevail, leaders need to 'ensure that individuals have low autonomy and decision-making latitude with the result that they are unaware how their individual contribution contributes to the overall goals and success of the organisation' (p. 187). If this is the case, then the advanced practitioner should mobilise a coachee's autonomy in the service of creating a positive coaching relationship.

PERSPECTIVES ON COMMITMENT

Helping a coachee to identify and strengthen her level of commitment to thinking differently or doing something new is a key element of what coaches do. Building commitment to action is a common element of coaching conversations, particularly towards the end of a session when the coachee is likely to be deciding on specific ways forward. However, a good outcome from a coaching conversation may not always, or exclusively, involve a clear and stated commitment to implementing a rational action plan that has emerged from the conversation. While the coachee may see logical and rational arguments for change, both those of her own making and those put forward by important stakeholders, a straightforward focus on the thinking or intellectual aspects of commitment may miss other vital factors that will impact significantly on her willingness or capability to follow through. These factors are likely to include emotional components that influence her motivation to implement the identified actions after the end of the coaching conversation. For example, significant personal and professional relationships could have a bearing on whether or not the coachee implements strategies that were discussed with her coach. It is important that any plans align with her values and the wider systemic features of the context in which she works. As Mary Beth O'Neill points out, 'Understanding is a necessary but insufficient criterion … Discussing obstacles and … reactions is a way that the [coachee] starts to imagine herself actually doing what it takes to accomplish the goal' (2007: 265).

Advanced practitioners are alert to these additional factors and notice subtle manifestations in a coachee's facial expressions, posture and breathing. Dale Schwarz and Anne Davidson (2009) highlight the requirement for a deep level of commitment to be present for someone to be purposefully active about a matter which is important to her. They refer to this as '"knowing in your bones" that what you are working toward is right and meaningful for you' (p. 242) and write about people 'living small – constraining their feelings and energy because of fear, a desire to fit in, to meet demands that others make of them, and for a host of other reasons' (p. 242). While acknowledging that the coachee's resulting body language can actually be a physical constraint on commitment, Schwarz and Davidson see a focus on changing the 'shapes' the body makes as a powerful, positive resource for driving personal change. Advanced practitioners should look for discrepancies between a coachee's stated purpose and how her body represents that purpose in a physical form and help her bring these two into alignment. Eunice Aquilina (2016) takes this thinking a step further in her exploration of somatic coaching. She suggests that people 'try to make sense of not knowing by seeking more information, looking inside ourselves for clarity, for a magical answer or a ready-made solution. And when that answer doesn't materialise we find ourselves, floundering, at sea. In our incessant quest for more information, more knowledge, we forget to pay attention to the person we are and how the answer we are so desperately searching for is not out there but resides within ourselves. In waking up to our own aliveness, we can go beyond cognitive knowing and begin to access a deeper wisdom that resides in each of us' (2016: 69).

Focus on practice: personal transition

Richard Strozzi-Heckler (2014, quoted in Aquilina, 2016: 67) identifies four phases to personal transition that are relevant for advanced practitioners:

1. Exploring the current historical situation – 'how we show up in our daily lives' as shaped by our history, including its physical manifestation represented by 'muscle memory' (p. 77).
2. Opening up and exploring the new unbounded possibilities – based on an acknowledgement of how our history generates our 'habitual way of being' and the extent to which our current 'adaptive strategies' are appropriate, or need to adapt to our new situation (p. 83).
3. Identifying a 'new shape' for thinking, feeling and behaving – resulting in a relinquishing of being shaped by the past in order to become more future-oriented, coupled with enhanced confidence to deal with the new scenario, and as yet unknown change going forward (p. 87).
4. Embodying this new shape into new routines – practising new behaviours and embedding learning, while remaining acutely alert to actions that supports the cultivation of the 'self we want to be in the world' (p. 88).

Aquilina points to the importance of enabling a coachee to 'declare a different future' (2016: 68) as a starting point for personal change. She also describes how, for major life changes, exploring the open, unbounded phase (Phase 2 above) can be both extremely challenging and rewarding. That sentiment is echoed in Clare McGregor's (2015) work with prisoners. Coaching Inside and Out is a charity that offers coaching to volunteer offenders who want to engage in conversations about making a significant change in their lives. In her inspiring book, McGregor describes the challenges involved in enabling coachees to build their commitment to make profound life changes. She points out that while the prison context is different to that encountered when coaching leaders and managers, many of the core issues about commitment are very similar. Indeed, some of our own coachees have spoken about feeling 'imprisoned' within their professional contexts.

PERSPECTIVES ON MOTIVATION

Much has been written about the power of intrinsic over extrinsic motivation. It is axiomatic that finding our inner motivation to perform and achieve has far greater impact on our ability to change than someone telling us to behave differently. Coaches often work with coachees to enable them to find their inner commitment even when driven by external, contextual factors. MacKie describes the three critical concepts of intrinsic motivation as autonomy, mastery and purpose: autonomy is defined as 'the drive to be self-directed'; mastery as 'the drive to keep improving at something that is important'; and purpose as 'the drive to connect our efforts to self-transcendent goals' (2016: 154). Positive psychologist Ilona Boniwell helpfully distinguishes three different types of motivation:

- Introjected motivation is based on self-control, acting in order to avoid guilt, pressure and anxiety. We do something because we would feel guilty if we didn't.
- Identified motivation means we do something because we can see why it is important (even though we don't enjoy it).
- Integrated motivation means we do something because we fully subscribe to the values underlying our behaviour, which have become part of ourselves. (2012: 65)

Aware of the different types of motivation, advanced practitioners will be able to work with their coachees to raise awareness about the benefits of undertaking tasks and behaviours that are fully integrated with their values. Not only will the coachees be more motivated, they will experience higher levels of wellbeing, too.

Reflections from experienced coaches: Motivation, culture and personal preferences

When coaching people in the creative industries, Jen Gash (2017) notes how different personalities tackle finding the commitment and energy to overcome obstacles. In most cases she identifies that, whatever their particular personal preference, often plunging in and 'having a go' is the precursor to stronger engagement. Then she notices that each small engagement with the process strengthens interest and creates and sustains 'flow' (Csikszentmihalyi, 1990) that is characterised in being so engaged that her coachees become separated from all else around them.

Gash points out that the term 'motivation' is 'laden with huge cultural meaning and is often used to berate ourselves or others for not doing something we say is important' (2017: 54). This 'language shortcut' (e.g. being diagnosed as 'not motivated') is 'often used harshly, thus expressing a lack of understanding of the complex factors' affecting how commitment gets turned into sustainable action (p. 54). Gash suggests that each encounter with a different coachee will involve a different combination of motivational factors, which need to be explored in order to be fully understood.

Novice coaches are trained to ensure that there is a clear goal for every coaching conversation. This makes sense in terms of enabling those new to coaching to work to a structured process which shifts them away from everyday default conversational habits. Normally, a goal is not an essential element of dialogue. Our discussion so far in this chapter suggests that establishing a distinct purpose at the outset of a coaching conversation may well involve a number of complexities that need to be explored for a clearer goal to emerge. David Clutterbuck proposes that 'over-adherence to goals in a coaching process is unhelpful' and in reality 'goals naturally emerge, shift and change' (quoted in Gash, 2017: 115).

Advanced practitioners are aware of the complexities involved and are flexible in assisting coachees to come to their own conclusions about purpose, direction and progress. They see goal-setting as part of a continuous contracting process throughout the coaching conversation and relationship. Part of this process involves helping coachees make choices about options.

In *The Art of Choosing*, Sheena Iyengar writes about the double-edged nature of choice in the modern era: 'We all know we want choice and like having options. The word "choice" almost always carries a positive connotation; conversely, to say "I had little or no choice" is usually to apologise or to explain one's unfortunately limited predicament. We assume that if having choice is good, having more must be better. For all its positive qualities, however, a wide variety of choice can also be confusing and overwhelming'

(2010: 179). In addition, being faced with too many choices can be de-motivating, and even paralysing in terms of taking action.

PERSPECTIVES ON PERSONAL CHANGE

Change is a permanent feature of modern life, whose acceleration seems to be on a continuous upward curve, not least as a result of rapid technological innovations. It is no surprise therefore that change is a frequent focus in coaching, even when it is not an explicit starting point for the coachee. Change is an area which has given birth to a plethora of research and publications. Coaches draw on a range of helpful models and frameworks to enable their coachees to address matters related to personal and organisational change (such as Kubler-Ross's stages of grief curve, Kotter's 8-step change model, Prochaska and Di Clemente's transtheoretical stages of change and Lewin's change management model). Such frameworks can be helpful in coaching. Some, like Kotter's, can seem rather mechanistic and descriptive. Others, like Kubler-Ross's stages of grief model has almost universal application to a diverse range of change situations beyond bereavement. No change model can capture all the intricacies of a particular instance of personal change. However, coachees frequently find features that resonate with their experience, helping them to understand their responses and how they might move forward positively.

William Bridges offers a helpful distinction between personal and organisational change. He refers to the former as 'transition' and the latter as 'transformation' (2009). He argues that while organisations may put effort and energy into designing and implementing a transformation programme, they often pay insufficient attention to how individuals and teams relate to the personal transition implications. Bridges describes three key phases of personal transition:

1. Ending, losing and letting go: 'Letting go of the old ways and the identity people had. This first phase of transition is an ending, and the time when [people need help] to deal with their losses.'
2. The neutral zone: 'an in-between time when the old is gone but the new isn't fully operational ... It's when the critical psychological realignments and re-patterings take place.'
3. The new beginning: this involves emerging out of the transition and it is when 'people develop the new identity, experience the new energy, and discover the new sense of purpose that make the change begin to work'. (2009: 4)

For Bridges, 'transition is a process by which people unplug from an old world and plug into a new world' so 'transition starts with an ending and ends with a beginning' (2009: 5). His use of the term 'neutral' for the second phase seems an insubstantial epithet to attach to a very complex and active part of personal change. Erik de Haan and Anthony Kasozi (2015) also delve into the complexities of transition as they relate to leadership in organisations. They point to the costs, in terms of money, health and wellbeing, the 'shadow sides' of leadership can create in individual leaders, for those they lead and for their organisations more widely. These shadow sides arise from the 'splits' that are the inevitable result of the leader's role. On the one hand there is the prestige, status and credibility associated with the leadership role for the individual inhabiting it. On the other hand, the very nature of the role causes the leader to be separated from those they lead. This separation 'offers the leader the unique opportunity to help others to make meaning ... The split symbolises and thus maintains a relationship, in which learning and development can take place, and action prepared' (p. 149).

De Haan and Kasozi suggest this split leads to a parallel split in the leader herself, which has an associated shadow side, 'a rift between their sunny, active, constructive, or aggressive side that has the ambition to contribute, create and prove something, and their doubting, pessimistic, needy, vulnerable, careful and concerned side, which craves connection with oneself and others' (p. 149). Most leaders, de Haan and Kasozi contend, keep their shadow sides hidden with potential negative impacts, such as derailment through overdrive and hubris, and related implications for their behaviour and wellbeing. Given this inner source of a leader's ineffectiveness is buried deep, it is difficult and challenging for her coach to enable them to be surfaced and addressed. That splits and rifts such as these have potentially damaging consequences for our mental health has long been an accepted tenet of eastern philosophies, which place more emphasis on 'going with the flow'.

In western society, people can find living with uncertainty problematic and feel the need to continually break things down into their constituent parts in order to understand them better, and in the process can lose sight of the vital connections between the constituent parts and how the whole fits into the wider system. 'We split ourselves from the "world out there", from each other, and then we proceed to split ourselves and the outside world into smaller clearly defined bits. What gets lost in this process is a sense of wholeness and oneness' (Kowalski, 2011, quoted in Hall, 2013: 144). Jennifer Plaister-Ten (2016) alerts coaches to the importance of working with world perspectives that a coachee brings into a coaching relationship. These need to be explored because they may be in tension with predominant cultural norms, and are also likely to be the source of important personal strengths for the coachee.

Focus on practice: Being tenacious and encouraging autonomy

So, what is emerging from this exploration about the advanced practice involved in being tenacious and encouraging autonomy in our coachees? Hawkins and Smith see the ability to 'encourage, motivate and carry appropriate optimism' as a core coaching skill (2006: 238). It seems clear that, as a result of the complexities involved, much of what the coachee may need to shine a light on, explore and address in order to make meaningful progress may be buried deep within her and beyond her immediate grasp. For example, she may be able to describe a set of factors that are the components of her intrinsic motivation but these may be generated from the perspective of her work role, rather than what she is really passionate about in her life. Work-based and life-based motivators may overlap to a greater or lesser degree. However, the coachee may find valuable insights in a deeper understanding of the extent of the congruence. Advanced practitioners will be alert to the coachee as a 'whole person' and not simply someone who performs a role and a set of functions for an organisation. Enabling the coachee to understand more of herself and her purpose will provide a strong foundation for her to build, consolidate and sustain her motivation. Inherent in this process will be the creation of a deeper understanding of the impacts on how she thinks, feels and behaves. The advanced practitioner encourages her coachee to muster as much control and influence as possible to 'live large', rather than 'live small' (Schwarz & Davidson, 2009: 242).

Advanced practitioners will challenge and test a coachee's commitment to enable her to gain a firm and clear sense of what she is really prepared to sign up to. This might involve helping clarity to emerge about what is known, what *needs* to be known and what can be left unknown. The organisational world is largely a rational, cognitive place with a thirst for information and knowledge. Coping positively with ambiguity and ignorance and feeling comfortable with the unknown is an essential, and increasingly important, contemporary capability for leaders, managers and coaches. Lindqvist (2002) suggests it is possible we may already know enough: 'It is not knowledge we lack. What is missing is the courage to understand what we know and to draw conclusions'.

Advanced practitioners have a crucial role in supporting and challenging coachees to identify and understand their motivation whilst also respecting their independence and autonomy. This requires a high level of noticing. The advanced practitioner must be attuned to the congruences and mis-alignment of her coachee's thinking, emotions and behaviour. How the coachee 'is' in the room becomes a prime source of assessing her readiness for change and her understanding of her own motivation. How the coachee 'shows up' is the most realistic and live 'data' available to the coach. The advanced practitioner is able to use her lived experience of the coachee to hold up a mirror and enable her to see and hear herself more accurately. While she does not coerce the coachee into acting, she is tenacious in encouraging her to move towards a positive outcome, whether that involves, for example, building commitment for following objectives through to implementation, gaining greater depth of understanding as a foundation for action or gaining insight related to awareness of the impact of her behaviour on others.

Coaching fits well into the expanding interest in conversational approaches in the organisational development field. As a prime example of the conversational philosophy, appreciative inquiry offers coaches a flexible, adaptable process for exploring personal transition and the connections to organisational transformation. The 4-D Framework (Discovery–Dream–Design–Destiny) (Cooperrider & Whitney, 2008) maps well onto coaching models, such as GROW (Whitmore, 2009), and provides a positive, future- and outcome-focused orientation for a coaching conversation.

Earlier in this chapter, we made reference to some change frameworks that are available to leaders and managers. Whether a coachee is aware of, and draws on, these theoretical underpinnings she will, no doubt, have her own personal 'theory of change'. This theory will underpin how she feels and thinks about change, and how she activates and responds to change initiatives. As Schwarz and Davidson point out, 'people's mental models drive behaviour' (2009: 79). The advanced practitioner enables a coachee to realise that she has a mental model about change which informs her thinking and behaviour. It is the coachee's role to acknowledge and understand its implications, to adjust it in ways she believes will meet the prevailing circumstances and decide whether or not to make the change.

It is important to note that enabling someone to be more autonomous will inevitably have impacts on the people around them. The advanced practitioner is aware of this and encourages her coachee to think through and plan for those impacts. There may be implications too for the coaching relationship. For example, the coach's desire to ensure that the coachee has complete autonomy may be in tension with a need (in the coach) for her to be making more progress than is apparent. The advanced practitioner makes a judgement about what constitutes an appropriate level of constructive challenge, which is in service of the coachee's overall stated purpose.

We have mentioned the complexities associated with the coachee's 'inner world'. Advanced practitioners are also acutely aware of the complexities related to the positioning of the coachee in a wider system. This means being alert to the impact she has on colleagues around her, in her team, department and organisation, and how this wider context affects her appetite for change. To varying degrees, dependent on role and relevance, the coachee's system may encompass people and functions beyond the organisation (e.g. social, technological, economic, environmental and political). Advanced practitioners enable their coachees to identify and work with what Whittington calls the 'hidden forces in systems' (2016: 18).

In conclusion, while the coachee is 'an autonomous individual who holds the answers to [her] questions' (Iordanou, 2017: 50), she may need encouragement and challenge to reach a point where she feels able to commit to action, especially when this involves major personal change. The advanced practitioner is able to read the verbal and physical signals that indicate readiness for change and remain appropriately tenacious in enabling her coachee to achieve her desired outcomes.

6
BEING CREATIVE AND PROTECTING TRUST

Visit https://study.sagepub.com/advancedcoaching to watch the videos discussed in this chapter:

VIDEO 6.1: Bringing creativity into a coaching session

VIDEO 6.2: Using storyboarding to help the coachee become unstuck

VIDEO 6.3: Using a creative technique to provide a new perspective

Management consultants John Ridderstråle and Kjell Nordström argue that the creativity and innovation required in organisations for humanity to survive and prosper will only emerge if people have the space, permission and time to make mistakes and experiment. According to them, 'instead of playing grown-ups, it is time for grown-ups to start playing' (2004: 182). Might being playful be a prerequisite for creativity and purposeful innovation? Given coaching is now recognised as a major leadership and management development activity, what are advanced practitioners doing to contribute to encouraging and mobilising the creativity of their coachees?

This is an area that has not received much attention in coaching publications until recently. Where writers' attention has focused on creativity it has tended to take the form of additional creative techniques that coaches can add to their repertoires to enable new insights to arise from different and unusual perspectives. However, this situation is changing with contributions to the field such as Jen Gash's book *Coaching Creativity* (2017), which focuses on galvanising people's creative impulses in the service of unleashing personal potential and stimulating enhanced performance.

We should begin by emphasising that we see *all* coaching activity as creative. We recognise the risk that by implying there are particular creative coaching approaches we may seem to suggest that there must therefore be 'non-creative' coaching interventions. On the contrary, asking a powerful question is a creative act. In engaging strongly with her coachee, a coach is using empathic listening creatively. In essence, what coaches and writers are doing when focusing on creativity in coaching is drawing on the plethora of possible perspectives that can be adopted from the world of the arts. This includes what coaches can make use of for the benefit of coachees from the visual arts, literature, sculpture, drama, comedy, music and so on. Just as the coaching profession has borrowed and adapted thinking and approaches from counselling, management theory, education, sports psychology and other fields, there is much to be gained by learning from, for example, art therapy, storytelling, actor training, and film and music production. Again, there is a caveat. Creativity is not the sole preserve of artists, musicians, writers and performers. Scientists, mathematicians and engineers are clearly creative in their own professional fields. There will be valuable insights to be gained from considering different cultural perspectives on what constitutes creativity in other communities.

Everyone will have their own perceptions about creativity and their own creative abilities. Some people would not describe themselves as being creative or may be reluctant to engage in 'creative' activities. As for applying creative interests and abilities in the workplace, this can often be portrayed as frivolous. Some would suggest that creativity can distract people from the business needs of their organisations. However, we would argue that we all have the potential to be creative. Advanced practitioners tap into this creativity to support their coachees to generate new ideas, become more engaged and experienced in order to enhance wellbeing in their professional contexts.

Curiosity is a crucial element of creativity. Ronald Heifetz and Marty Linsky (2002) describe how curiosity and an associated humble acknowledgement of what we *don't* know are discouraged in many organisations: 'The dynamic starts early. By the time children reach adolescence, they already form deep attachments to having it "right". They begin to lose that wonderful curiosity that comes from knowing what they do not know, when they assume people with a different point of view are there to learn from, not just argue with. But the sense of mystery and wonder so precious in the early years fades fast as the routine debates develop the characteristic structure: "I'm right", "No, I'm right!", "No I'm right!"' (p. 233). Further, organisational cultures can signal that creativity is not valued. In their book *Living Leadership*, George Binney, Gerhard Wilke and Colin Williams argue that a rigid adherence to targets closes down 'the space for creativity' (2009: 262).

Dan Roam (2008) writes about peoples' different perspectives on visual thinking and drawing. 'Black-pen people', he says, are those who can't resist sketching when opportunities arise and comprise about 25 per cent of the population. A further 50 per cent are 'yellow-pen people', who are focused on highlighting and commenting on others' visual creations. 'Red-pen people' make up the other quarter of the population and think that visual representations are at best an over-simplification of complex realities. Some coachees will come to sessions with these kinds of perceptions about creativity. So how do advanced practitioners enable them to consider the benefits of exploring things from radically different perspectives? How do they introduce the concept of creativity into their work to maintain and strengthen the trust that coachees have in the process and in the coaching relationship?

Van Nieuwerburgh (2017) highlights the importance of encouraging coachees to be creative, in particular generating activities that move beyond the cognitive and a focus on talk alone. In the contemporary world of work, thinking and talking are staple features of organisational life and it is likely the coachee will have already applied her default ways of tackling her challenge before she has entered the coaching room. This means her coach needs to help her find new ways to approach her situation, which, as van Nieuwerburgh points out, are likely to lie beyond her usual comfort zones and preferred learning styles (p. 181).

See it in practice: Being creative in coaching conversations

In some of the coaching videos that accompany this book, the coach introduces a creative technique. For example, using his coachee's language, Bob encourages his coachee to explore juxtaposing archetypes ('Cool, collected Lina' and 'Hot mess Lina'), which allow her to see her challenges from two contradictory perspectives (see Video 6.1). Helen uses a storyboarding technique with her coachee to enable her to visualise her goal and see the milestones towards its achievement (see Video 6.2). David uses different coloured sticky notes to help his coachee to capture and explore the benefits and drawbacks of her behaviour at work (see Video 6.3).

Video 6.1

Video 6.2

Video 6.3

PERSPECTIVES ON CREATIVITY

So what is creativity? According to Jill Badonsky, 'creativity is a puzzle and a paradox' (2010: 21). 'Artists, writers, scientists, rarely know how their original ideas arise so there may never be a scientific theory of creativity. The apparent unpredictability of creativity defies any scientific explanation or prescribed formula' (p. 21). Psychologist Mihaly Csikszentmihalyi (1990) studied creative people and discovered that 'creativity generally involves crossing boundaries and domains' (in Pink, 2005: 135). For Daniel Pink, this boundary-spanning involves 'the most creative among us [seeing] relationships the rest of us never notice' (2005: 135).

David Sibbet uses the analogy of structural tension in engineering to illustrate how people tackle tensions between their ambition and their reality: 'Humans resolve ... tension by either compromising on their visions or changing current reality (or not connecting the two). Creative people have an appetite for creative tension and hold their visions while exploring every possible way to change reality' (2010: 169). The tension can manifest itself in cognitive dissonance in the individual and inertia in the system in which they operate. In both situations it can be easier to leave things as they are, however uncomfortable that may be. 'Highly creative people have the capacity to keep themselves in this space of creative tension long enough that they coax extraordinary results from the physical resources they have to work with' (p. 169).

For coaches Dale Schwarz and Anne Davidson, creativity is 'perceiving and applying things in different ways' (2009: 340). This involves reconfiguring existing knowledge and theories and noticing the interconnectedness of things and ideas. They point out, in line with David Clutterbuck's thinking about diversity (2007), that creativity is more likely to be generated by the interplay of difference, which brings other ways of perceiving to the table. Mobilising creative thinking and activity can, however, be 'much more difficult when rigid limitations are placed on what is "possible" or when certain results are expected' (Schwarz & Davidson, 2009: 340). Essentially, creativity often arises from 'mistakes'. Schwarz and Davidson also suggest that creativity is 'enhanced and set free when you nurture and respect your inner self' (p. 340).

Margaret Wheatley and Myron Kellner-Rogers ask 'What has kept us from seeing life as creative, even playful?' (1996: 11). They cite Darwinism as one major foundation of a belief that the emergence of human life, indeed that of all species, was accidental with 'lucky genetic errors' surviving. Such thinking, they argue, has positioned us in perpetual conflict with an environment which we perceive as hostile to our existence, rather than seeing a world 'which is continually exploring and creating ... We are here to create, not defend' (p. 11). Wheatley and Kellner-Rogers outline how 'images of life as creative and playful have been with us for thousands of years in many spiritual traditions, but modern Western thought makes it difficult to approach life as play ... All of us are always engaged in trying to convey our experience of life in images that connect it with other experiences ... We create metaphors to connect what we see' (p. 12). They quote the French philosopher, Henri Bergson, who said: 'I believe I experience creativity at every moment of my life' (p. 13).

Wheatley and Kellner-Rogers suggest a set of principles that underlie life's creativity:

- everything is in a constant process of discovering and creating
- life uses messes to get to well-ordered solutions
- life is intent on finding what works, not what's 'right'
- life creates more possibilities as it engages with opportunities. (1996: 13)

Advanced practitioners would consider these principles about creativity to be an essential part of coaching. In fact, such principles can be seen to underpin effective, transformational coaching conversations.

Daniel Pink argues that 'for nearly a century Western society ... has been dominated by a form of thinking and an approach to life that is narrowly reductive and deeply analytical' (2005: 2). For Pink, creative thinking is now *the* critical factor for organisational success. Nancy Kline (1999) highlights the importance of a culture that encourages serious thinking and reflection as precursors to the emergence of creativity. This idea is echoed in Ilona Boniwell's writings about positive psychology: 'What is important is the organisational atmosphere that encourages following hunches and using intuitive understanding, supports innovative ideas, provides resources and facilitates networking' (2012: 155). Designer Clement Mok (Mok, personal communication) is adamant the future 'will require people to think and work across boundaries into new zones that are totally different from their areas of expertise. They will not only have to cross those boundaries, but they will also have to identify opportunities and make connections between them' (in Pink, 2005: 135). It is clear that our world will continue to evolve at a rapid pace increasing its level of complexity. People and organisations will therefore continue to be presented with intense challenges, many of which they will not be able to predict. Finding creative ways of addressing the leadership, organisational and societal impacts of these emerging challenges will be essential.

As Gash (2017) points out, defining the term 'creativity' can be problematic, not least because it has different sociological and historical interpretations. She sees the pursuit of a detailed and precise definition as potentially a distraction for coaches and urges advanced practitioners to give thought to what the term means to them as individuals and to the associated implications for coaching. Helpfully, she quotes James Kaufmann on the difficulties of describing terminology, 'creativity' being

> much more than a basic definition and the concept of divergent thinking. When I talk about creativity, am I talking about a beautiful piece of art or an ingenious computer program? How about the sensation of the 'a-ha' process where I suddenly understand what I need to do next? Maybe, instead, I'm talking about how a creative person behaves. Or maybe it's the synergy that happens when many different people share and exchange ideas together. Throwing all of these things together and labelling them as 'creativity' is not much different than using the word 'love' to mean your feelings for your mom, your best friend, your significant other, and spicy calamari. It may be technically correct, but it's not terribly useful. (in Gash, 2017: 5)

In focusing on creativity in this chapter we will be using Gash's proposed working definition: 'creativity = bringing something new into being' (2017: 5). From our review of the concept in this chapter, this idea of 'newness' emerges from a level of comfort with uncertainty or 'not knowing' alongside an ability to make connections and think across traditional boundaries.

Focus on practice: Co-creating the conditions for using creative approaches in coaching

Michael Ray and Rochelle Myers identify the principles underpinning creativity as:

- faith in your own creativity
- absence of negative judgement
- precise observation
- penetrating questioning. (1986: 10)

Advanced practitioners can certainly help coachees with the last three points. They are also adept at not judging their coachees and can transfer this mindset and skill to coachees' creative endeavours. Equally, asking powerful questions and encouraging precision in noticing the impacts of thinking and behaviour are central to the practice of coaching. For all the reasons previously outlined we will encounter coachees who lack faith in their own creative abilities or are adamant that they have no skill in this area. Consequently, such coachees can be very uncomfortable with 'soft and fluffy' activities. It is here that coaches are likely to encounter the most challenges. So, how might we help coachees overcome doubts about their own creativity?

Ellen Langer asserts that 'understanding how to think mindfully is the best way to break through the roadblocks that keep us from developing our creative selves. When we are mindfully creative, we are authentic; we're not being reactive but acting according to our own scripts. We can be original and liberated from doing things "the right way"' (quoted in Hall, 2013: 195). Mindfulness is a powerful tool to help stop the self-criticism and keep the creative juices flowing. Mindlessness 'freezes our responses and closes us off to the possibility of change' (p. 197). In this state, Hall asserts that we underestimate the energy and insight uncertainty can generate, in part because organisational cultures pressure us to do all we can to liberate ourselves from not knowing, which is the foundation of mindlessness. Hall refers to research (Colzato et al., 2012) which indicates that mindfulness and meditation promote the divergent thinking that is a key source of new ideas (Hall, 2013: 199).

In the section below, we will focus on one particular aspect of creativity in coaching: using visual thinking and sketching. We believe the principles and practices here are applicable and transferable to other creative approaches that coaches might deploy.

Visual thinking is a vital feature of human interaction with the world. Images bring ideas to life, and captivating speakers embed visual imagery in their oratory to create powerful emotional connections. A prime example is Martin Luther King's 'I have a dream' speech. Pictures make ideas more real and accessible, which is one reason leaders establish 'visions' to illustrate their organisation's ambitions. They know that building emotional linkages which integrate the head and the heart can enable people to visualise a different future. Visual imagery can also have a profoundly cathartic effect. One of us witnessed the terrorist attack on a London bus on 7 July 2005 and as an avid amateur cartoonist used sketching to overcome the subsequent psychological distress.

In the field of design, Colin Ware (2008) indicates the vital importance of scribbling as a foundation stone in creating aesthetic and functional buildings and objects. Designers, he writes, frequently illustrate an initial rough idea for a design with a scribbled sketch which provides the basis for an initial critique, leading to refinements in the design. Without the scribble, the critiquing process is rendered much more difficult: 'The deliberately 'random' scribble is often used by artists and designers as a way of liberating their creative process from stereotypical visual thinking. [Our] perceptual mechanisms are exquisitely tuned to find meaning often from slender evidence and this is why meaning is so readily found in meaningless scribbles' (p. 154). The scribbling process is elliptical and involves:

- a vague concept
- a loose scribble on paper
- adding marks to extend or consolidate the design
- visually scanning and constructively interpreting the scribble
- mentally projecting additions to the scribble
- adding marks to extend or consolidate the design (p. 159).

Roam suggests that 'solving problems with pictures has nothing to do with artistic training or talent' (2008: 4). Essentially, visual problem-solving involves making decisions with less-than-perfect information and a visual language that is made up of a small number of elements, such as circles, squares, lines and curves. The process of visual thinking is based on four phases: looking, seeing, imagining and representing (Roam, 2008). This process mirrors those aspects of the GROW model (Whitmore, 1992) that focus on the current reality and future options.

But the use of creative approaches in coaching is not just about helping a coachee solve a problem in an innovative way. Mobilising a coachee's creativity can create the conditions for her to achieve a state of 'flow' – the positive psychological state of being fully engaged and lost in an activity (Csikszentmihalyi, 1990) – which in turn allows for a sense of freedom and liberation. In this state the coachee is more likely to access different ways of thinking about her issue, enhancing her analytical capabilities.

(Continued)

(Continued)

For Lowe, 'visual prompts can bypass the language area of the brain and connect to a place of being more creative. This can provide new insights and new information and can almost dethrone the rational mind during the coaching' (Lowe, personal communication in Seignot, 2016: 49). Creative approaches, being playful, offer a more relaxed mode from which insight and learning may emerge. Coaches often use creative methods when coachees have become stuck. Quoted in an article in *Coaching at Work* magazine, David Clutterbuck urges coaches to be clear about the reasons for using creative approaches and to be certain that it is because the coachee, rather than the coach herself, is blocked (personal communication in Seignot, 2016: 49).

Reflections from experienced coaches: Sketching

Anna Sheather (2017) is a coach who uses sketching in coaching very effectively. She writes that 'art allows us to work beyond words, connecting our clients to a much deeper level of personal awareness, understanding and meaning ... A deeper level of connection that brings transformational shift' (p. 48). She asserts that it is all about personal expression. According to her experience of sketching during coaching conversations, shifts can emerge by:

- allowing clients to externalise those things they find difficult to verbalise
- enabling complexity and paradox to be held simultaneously, creating a safe and easier space to explore what can be frustrating and unsettling
- allowing clients to connect with embodied emotions through the physical process of creating art; emotions that can then be explored through the created image
- unlocking hidden material quickly, fast tracking to the core issue and our work together
- breaking out of thought loops and stuck ways of thinking
- creating visual outputs that are memorable and 'keepable', enabling coach and client to return to them, exploring changes, and uncovering emerging meanings, patterns and themes. Words, by contrast, can often be forgotten, misremembered and reshaped (p. 48).

Sheather's suggested applications can be used by advanced practitioners to bring creativity into coaching conversations. A coach can further facilitate her coachee's creative thinking and its representation through sketching by encouraging her to pursue the wildest, off-the-wall hunches in which might lie the kernel of a new way of understanding.

Stories from our practice: Using sketches and cartoons

In our own practice we have seen how sketching and cartooning have helped coachees in a number of ways – from gaining a different and deeper understanding of a specific challenge, through exploring the emotional elements of their relationships with significant others at work, to identifying concrete ways forward through a complex situation because they have accessed different ways of seeing the issues. We know coachees who display the resulting sketches and refer back to them as a continuous source of inspiration and comfort, and others who have used the sketches to stimulate important conversations with their teams and other work colleagues. Sometimes, in-the-moment, rough-and-ready sketches and cartoons drawn by our coachees can end up decorating the refrigerator door at their homes or their desks at work!

According to Mark Williams and Danny Penman, 'The spirit in which you do something is often as important as the act itself ... If you do something in a negative or critical way, if you over-think or worry or carry out a task through gritted teeth, then you will activate your mind's aversion system. This will narrow the focus of your life. You will become like a mouse with an owl complex; more anxious, less flexible, less creative. If, however, you do exactly the same thing in an open-hearted, welcoming manner, you thereby activate the mind's "approach" system: your life has a chance to become richer, warmer, more flexible, and more creative' (2011: 114). For David Caruso and Peter Salovey (2004) too, such positive emotions facilitate the expansion of thinking, leading to the creation of novel ideas and encouraging the consideration of a wide range of possibilities. All this means that an advanced practitioner can help her coachee by encouraging a safe space and a positive mindset to support the creation of her sketch.

Inevitably, a coachee will make 'mistakes' in her sketch. So how does the advanced practitioner create a sense of safety and help her to stay motivated and connected with the process of sketching? According to Langer there are four main responses to such a mistake:

- throw the picture away because we can't bear mistakes
- opt to live with the mistake
- try to fix the mistake and get back towards our original intention
- reconsider the mistake and decide to make the most of it. (in Hall, 2013: 197)

Langer says it is this fourth position that brings us most of what we value in art but that culturally we are conditioned to consider only the first three possibilities (in Hall, 2013).

Ultimately, as Badonsky suggests, a coach needs to help her coachee give herself permission to go beyond her anxieties about creativity, which she describes as 'the ultimate growth process' (2010: 21). Badonsky points out that those very anxieties may actually be an indication that learning and development is taking place. 'The skills that we obtain by saying "yes" to the creative process are skills we can use in all areas of our lives: (e.g.) flexibility, intuition, risk-taking, confidence, playfulness, open-mindedness, resourcefulness, acceptance' (p. 21).

BUILDING AND PROTECTING TRUST

Trust is an essential ingredient in the relationship between coach and coachee, upon which the effectiveness of all coaching activity ultimately depends. The level of trust in coaching relationships is seriously challenged in the moment a coach introduces a way of working that takes her coachee far out of her comfort zone. Of course, this is not the case for all coachees, some of whom may relish the opportunity to engage in a novel approach. Handled carefully, any increased vulnerability arising from the coachee being taken further and further away from her comfort zone is likely to strengthen the level of trust in the relationship because the coach's respect and compassion will have a positive impact on how she is experienced.

The professional perspective: Role of trust

The International Coach Federation (ICF, 2017) emphasises the importance of trust in their competency framework.

'Establishing trust and intimacy with the client – ability to create a safe and supportive environment that produces ongoing mutual respect and trust:

a.   shows genuine concern for the client's welfare and future
b.   continuously demonstrates personal integrity, honesty and sincerity
c.   establishes clear agreements and keeps promises
d.   demonstrates respect for the client's perceptions, learning style, personal being
e.   provides on-going support for and champions new behaviours and actions, including those involving risk taking and fear of failure
f.   asks permission to coach client in sensitive, new areas.'

As Ian Blakey (2016) points out, trust can be a difficult concept to define with precision. He cites a number of research projects that identify three core components of trust:

- It involves taking a risk
- It involves keeping a positive expectation that the other party will not let you down; and
- It has rational, emotional and moral elements (p. 39).

Ioanna Iordanou and her co-writers (2017) underline the importance of emotional and moral elements in their focus on ethics in coaching. They point to the co-creation of trust as a vital and mutual activity that helps the coachee to have faith in her coach and emphasise the importance of the relationship embodying relevant personal as well as professional elements (p. 56). The coach then, needs to work in a genuine way through, for example, appropriate levels of self-disclosure. In this way she will enable her coachee to be confident in her level of coaching skill and to believe that wherever the conversation is going and however challenging it becomes, she will remain safe.

Blakey, writing about authentic leadership, identifies three 'pillars' of trust:

1. Ability: the 'professional competence to fulfil the core task ... delivering results'
2. Integrity: 'the extent to which we "walk the talk" ... being reliable in our behaviours and consistently living up to the values and standards we have set for ourselves'
3. Benevolence: 'our concern for the wellbeing of others'. (2016: 42)

Flores (2012) notes four factors that inform people's judgements about others' trustworthiness:

- Sincerity – does this person mean what they say? Is the way I experience them consistent with their intentions?
- Competence – does this person have the skills, resources and the capacity to do what they have committed to?
- Reliability – does this person take care of the situation and me consistently over time?
- Engagement – does this person care about what is important to me? Are they open to listening to my concerns? (in Aquilina, 2016: 116)

Eunice Aquilina suggests that a foundation stone for trust-building is a person's presence and the perceived congruence of 'mood, emotions, thoughts and actions' (2016: 112). She quotes Albert Mehrabian's research into trustworthiness, which indicates that when language and feelings are not congruent, body language and tone have significantly more impact than the spoken words. In addition, Jennifer Plaister-Ten alerts the coach to how the meanings and experience of trust can vary considerably in different cultures, suggesting that clarity is required in coaching conversations about what is understood by the term 'trust' and its implications for the relationship (2016: 112).

Alison Hardingham (2004) applies David Maister's framework for trust-building in professional relationships to coaching. The framework identifies four core elements: 'credibility, reliability, intimacy and perceived self-orientation' (p. 64). In introducing creative methods, a coach's credibility may be on the line. Her coachee needs to believe that the coach has faith in the method to produce benefits for her. In addition, the coach's reliability is tested; for instance, in adhering to the contracted conditions about keeping her safe in uncharted waters. Comfort, or intimacy, with the coach will also be a concern of the coachee, who will need to feel that the coach's behaviour is not out of sync with previous experience of her. Finally, the coachee will be seeking expressed signals that the coach cares about her (i.e. displays a lack of self-orientation), particularly in this potentially challenging moment (p. 64). Hardingham also points to the potential for damaging the four elements, thus undermining the trust in the coaching relationship.

In building the coachee's confidence in her, the coach must also, of course, trust in her own capacity to create and maintain a supportive and challenging learning environment. In turn, the projection of her own professional confidence will help the coachee to be confident in working with the coach, which will strengthen the degree of trust between them. Sustaining trust is a continuous process which can take the form of a virtuous or a vicious cycle depending on the intentions and behaviours of the coach and coachee, and the extent to which the latter feels empowered by her engagement with the coach. Brockbank and McGill describe the damaging effects when a vicious cycle starts to emerge.

> If the client feels powerless in a learning relationship, then there will be a lack of trust. Lack of trust means that the client will not feel able to trust the learning context, or any enabler of learning in that context. Given that reflective learning will involve feelings or emotion in addition to thinking and action, a lack of trust will inhibit any display of emotion or vulnerability and therefore openness to learning. When we really learn, particularly that which is potentially developmental, we lay ourselves open to uncertainty and can feel (temporarily) unstable. For the feelings that uncertainty can engender we need conditions of safety that ensure those expressed feelings are not taken advantage of. (2012: 35)

So what are the practical implications for a coach who feels her coachee might benefit from engaging with creative methods? As always with coaching, a fundamental factor is clear and explicit contracting, which includes consideration of learning styles, ways of working together and acknowledgement that there will almost certainly be times when an activity feels discomforting. Establishing a clear contract at the outset provides the coach with a reference point to return to in her introduction of a novel approach. The advanced practitioner will be contracting continuously throughout the coaching relationship, and this allows for the in-the-moment agreement about using a creative method. She will also be adept at creating the conditions for safe exploration, regardless of how challenging the subject matter and approach might turn out to be. An advanced practitioner is also likely to make it clear to her coachee that it is within the latter's power to call a halt to proceedings at any time, while simultaneously being sensitively persuasive about the insights that might yet accrue from continuing with the method.

Reflections from experienced coaches: Principles of creativity

It is worth coaches bearing in mind the underpinning principles for creativity that Badonsky describes:

- We were born with an affinity towards a particular creative talent that allows us to share with others something unique about ourselves.
- We have something that is uniquely our own to say, depict, or demonstrate, and thus we contribute variation, interest, and new dimension to the world.
- There is an audience for our art, no matter what form it takes. Finding what channel of expression is uniquely ours, gives us creative flow and flight, if we do not compare ourselves with what and how others have chosen to express themselves. If we are working with who we truly are in our own way, comparison becomes unimportant.
- The process of creativity produces optimal conditions for being alive. As we create, our minds and bodies are at their most energetic, stay vital, and even heal.
- Our self-esteem rises, our confidence deepens, our coping skills strengthen, and life becomes easier and more enjoyable. (2010: 22)

Paul Brown and Denyse Busby-Earle (2014) suggest a coach should help her coachee achieve a sense of 'wonder' through experiencing the 'startle/surprise' emotion. Harnessing coachees' creativity can provide just that surprise element, with coachees intrigued by what is emerging from the process that they could not see through simply talking about the issue. Paying attention to the imagery in her coachee's language and the connections with the imagery in her sketch can produce a sense of wonder causing powerful insights to be released. Encouraging coachees to think like cartoonists, for example, can help them to identify the most salient points – and inject some humour into the process (even if sometimes dark) to produce new and profound insights. An interesting by-product of using a creative approach in coaching is that the focus on a 'third party' (e.g. a picture, sketch or constellation) often creates the space for the coachee to talk in a more open way, especially about emotions, than when eye contact with the coach is more directly maintained.

For Jen Gash (2017), coaching is frequently overly focused on thinking and doing, ruling out the insights coachees can gain from different ways of seeing. In the foreword to her book, Bob Garvey (2017: xiii) draws on the ancient Greek notions of *techne* (scientific thinking, pre-planned learning) and *phronesis* (attentiveness, creativity) pointing to the downsides of the former, which might lead, for example, to inflexible competency frameworks and mechanistic assessment procedures on coaching qualification programmes. A balance of *techne* and *phronesis* is vital, so Gash suggests coaches should pay more attention to *phronesis*, which would emphasise intuition, wonder and insight on the part of both the coachee and the coach. She writes that both concepts have an important role to play in coaching, and neglecting *phronesis* means coaches are less likely to work with coachees as whole human beings. Mobilising creative energies opens a door into noticing and working with the feelings and values that underpin thinking and doing.

Clearly coaching involves conversation, which means a pre-eminent focus on words. Coaches frequently work with coachees who get stuck for words and are unable to get a grasp on how to accurately communicate their challenges or the associated emotions. Tapping into coachees' creativity can generate ways of overcoming the obstacles. Peter Greenaway, the film director, asserts that most films simply illustrate a story where words continue to be the main vehicle for communicating meaning (Greenaway, personal communication, quoted in Brown, 2016). Greenaway strives to create encounters with film where visual imagery plays a more major role than the words. In pursuing a similar theme of relying less on words as the sole means through which coachees describe their challenges, perhaps advanced practitioners can become even more impactful.

7

BEING ETHICAL AND STAYING TRUE TO PERSONAL VALUES

Visit https://study.sagepub.com/advancedcoaching to watch the video discussed in this chapter:

VIDEO 7.1: Withholding judgement

Stories from our practice: When values are challenged

It was a new experience for me. Aside from freelance coaches, I had never coached anyone from the private sector. I was asked if I would work with 'Jill' who had recently been made redundant from the finance sector and was increasingly bewildered by her position and confused as to why she was not readily securing a new job given her extensive expertise and experience. As most of my coaching to date had been with senior and middle managers in the public service, I had some trepidation about working with someone from outside this field but the coachee's situation involved some urgency time-wise. I was available and I reminded myself of my firm belief that coaching can have profound benefits regardless of a coachee's background. This belief was borne out by the eventual outcomes of the coaching relationship.

However, in the first session with Jill I noticed a reticence from her to engage, which caused me to feel uncomfortable. It became clear that she was very demoralised and distressed that, as the main breadwinner, her loss of income threatened the security of her family. I noticed how Jill's doubts about her future were influencing my disposition, ratchetting up my empathic response and undermining my usual positivity. I became acutely aware of the contrast between our situations with the juxtaposition of our different economic circumstances looming large in my mind.

The projection of Jill's despair to me was at first paralysing. Her self-belief was extremely low and I could feel this actively undermining my capacity to help. I sensed that I was losing touch with my own experience and expertise, exacerbated by encroaching doubts about my credibility as a 'public service' coach entering

(Continued)

(Continued)

an entirely new field. I began to wonder whether Jill's reticence was related to a perception of me as insufficiently experienced in her sector. I began to feel frustrated at my own inability to see how to help Jill move beyond her despair and, if I'm very honest, some irrational irritation with her for 'putting me in this position'.

I realised that there was something else happening. Alongside being 'caught' by Jill's desperation I wondered to what extent my public service values and political perspective were interfering with the progress of the coaching and crucially, in creating the most productive relationship for the coachee. I have mellowed with age but retain a very strong affinity with left-of-centre political thinking. I am critical of the banking sector for causing the financial crash of 2008 and the subsequent crisis that has led to austerity in the public sector. With hindsight I can see that this backdrop may have influenced this relationship with someone from the world of finance.

I am aware that Jill has not caused the cuts in public services and I empathise with her personal predicament. She recounted numerous stories of poor treatment she had encountered in some finance companies. One of my 'red buttons' relates to how people are treated in workplaces and what counts as reasonable and fair behaviour. Of course, these stories only added to my negative perception of the finance sector. I was drawn towards Jill as an individual, while feeling discomfited by the wider context in which she wished to continue to work.

How do we as coaches stay true to our own values? Is it even necessary that we do so? In her book on mindfulness in coaching, Liz Hall suggests that coaches may often feel they have to leave their 'true selves' at home (2013: 173). Does this matter if our role is to facilitate learning and development in others in their particular context? Does coaching have a wider societal role, contributing to some vision of a better future?

Taking this further, to what degree should a coach accept unquestioningly the values of her coachee? What ethical responsibility does a coach have to challenge her coachee's values where these appear 'inappropriate'? Who defines what is 'appropriate'? And on what grounds and principles, and with what authority? Those 'inappropriate' values might align well with the coachee's context. Is coaching simply about helping clients to be better at what they do? If that's the case, where do we draw the line (if at all) in deciding that a particular coaching contract is not to be entered into? In an admittedly extreme example, should we coach a military leader to take forward a policy which has dire consequences for a civilian population? Might her engagement with coaching also be a stimulus for a change of view, and what has her coach to do to spark a change of thinking? And is that the role of a coach anyway?

See it in practice: Withholding judgement

Video 7.1

In this video, Christian draws on the coachee's existing understanding of cultural factors that may be in play at work. The coach maintains a non-judgemental, curious approach throughout.

In the next chapter, we will explore how coaches can be authentic when working with their coachees. An important element of this authenticity involves remaining true to one's own values as a coach. In this chapter we will explore the complex ethical dimensions associated with attempting to achieve this aim. We are particularly interested in the ethics associated with not imposing one's personal values on others.

PERSPECTIVES ON ETHICS

We are taking as read that a coach must act ethically in all aspects of her work, from the quality of the relationship established with her coachee, through the methods she uses in working with that coachee to the activities that she engages in with sponsors and other stakeholders. Indeed, the Association for Coaching, the European Mentoring and Coaching Council and the International Coach Federation have well-rehearsed ethical codes to which their members are expected to adhere. For example, the International Coach Federation addresses this matter in the 'Professional Conduct at Large' section of their Code of Ethics:

> As a coach I ... strive at all times to recognise my personal issues that may impair, conflict with or interfere with my coaching performance or my professional coaching relationships. I will promptly seek the relevant professional assistance and determine the action to be taken, including whether it is appropriate to suspend or terminate my coaching relationship(s) whenever the facts and circumstances necessitate. (ICF, 2015: Part 2, Point 8)

However, as a number of discussions about coaches' ethical behaviour indicate (e.g. Passmore & Turner, 2018; Passmore, Csigsas & Brown, 2017), there are considerable differences in how individual coaches approach ethically challenging situations.

Perhaps this is unsurprising given that there is rarely an absolute 'right' or 'wrong' position to take with an ethical issue, which will be influenced by a range of complex factors, such as, for example, cultural and societal norms, and individuals' personal views on such matters. It does, however, point concerningly to the potential ambiguity of ethical practice in coaching. In addition, by their nature, ethical issues tend to emerge as dilemmas (where responses have to be continually managed and adjusted to take account of changing circumstances), rather than as simple problems (which might be amenable to a once-and-for-all solution). Many writers in the field have made eloquent cases for this position, and acknowledge that, as with ethical considerations in all facets of life, coaches should view the issues that arise as dilemmas rather than problems.

While accepting the importance of managing ethical considerations, van Nieuwerburgh (2017) challenges the use of the term 'dilemma' on the grounds that it imputes a negative connotation to ethical questions. Further, the word implies that there are only two ways of proceeding, when such thinking may get in the way of considering a broad range of possible courses of action. Besides, he suggests, we need to see 'ethical moments of choice' as critical moments in a coaching conversation which provide opportunities for growth for the coachee (and the coach) (pp. 192–3). This chimes with De Haan's (2008) ideas about 'critical moments' in coaching. He defines a critical moment as a significant moment that says something crucial about the coachee, the coach and their relationship, and has the potential to generate profound insights.

Van Nieuwerburgh (2017) proposes a 'cycle of ethical maturity' as a process for coaches to use to enhance their practice. According to this cycle, an advanced practitioner's confidence in her own deeply held values and principles allows her to be more open to ethical moments of choice. In turn, this openness to moments of choice means that an advanced practitioner can make the courageous decisions to address ethical issues when they arise. Once ethical issues have been addressed, the advanced practitioner would reflect (after the session) on how she managed the moment of choice and consider what she learned through the experience. This reflective practice leads to increased ethical maturity which builds the advanced practitioner's confidence in her own values and principles. This is the point at which the cycle returns to its starting point. The cycle of ethical maturity is a virtuous cycle in that the process reinforces itself and leads to further positive growth and development (p. 197). We believe regular and reflective practice is a crucial undertaking if coaches are to develop the intricate sensitivities required to be able to work with the diverse nature of humanity. Taking inclusion and diversity as a point of focus, Thompson (2017) emphasises the importance of *critical* reflective practice for surfacing ideological or dogmatic assumptions that are insensitive, discriminatory, offensive or oppressive that can leak into our language and imagery. He urges guarding against reflection becoming simply 'a routine'. The reflection process 'needs to be critical, in the sense of not taking existing social arrangements for granted, not making assumptions that can legitimate, reinforce or accentuate existing patterns of inequality' (p. 242, our emphasis).

De Jong notes that ethical maturity involves placing integrity at the heart of coaching work, a notion that has 'connotations of incorruptibility, soundness, completeness, honesty, sincerity, fairness and straightforwardness of conduct' (2010: 210). Given ethics can be seen as the codification of acceptable moral behaviour, he concludes that coaches do have the capabilities, knowledge and professional support (in the form of codes of ethics and supervision opportunities) to be ethical but questions whether this necessarily means that we can be moral. In synthesising a range of different definitions, de Jong concludes that 'ethics calls for moral practice [and] takes on its fullest sense when we translate theories into moral principles that can be used as drivers towards ideal ends' (p. 206). He notes that 'values play an important part in ethical decision-making. Values are based upon our belief systems about what is *desirable* [our emphasis], rather than what is right or wrong' (p. 206). Further, 'to be ethical means one is able to differentiate between acts that are good and those that are bad. What one does after that differentiation is made, is what determines whether or not we are moral persons. After all, distinguishing right from wrong is one thing – but to actually do what we believe to be right, and to refrain from doing what we believe to be wrong is quite another' (p. 206).

Brennan and Wildflower's survey of codes of ethics (2010) identifies five key underpinning principles:

1. Do not cause harm to others.
2. Act in ways that promote the welfare of others.
3. Know the limits of your competence and work within these.
4. Respect the interests of the client.
5. Respect the law.

Using a transactional analysis (TA) perspective, Julie Hay sees the principles behind ethical coaching practice as:

•   everyone operates within their own unique map of the world
•   people are not the same as their behaviours
•   all behaviours have a positive intention
•   we cannot not communicate – there is always the possibility of leakage. (2007: 126)

Simon Cavicchia and Maria Gilbert (2019) critique traditional views of ethics by asserting that it is based on a series of inadequate assumptions about how human beings behave.

They quote Mattingly (2005), who presents the following assumptions:

1.   It is possible to articulate universal ethical principles or guidelines that are useful in every situation. Ethical rules are context free.
2.   There is always an ethical 'right answer'.
3.   There is an objective position from which to judge what one ought to do. The position is characterised by emotional detachment from the situation.
4.   This objectively defined position, without any emotional involvement, enables the articulation of unambiguous ethical guidelines. (in Cavicchia & Gilbert, 2019: 206)

Cavicchia and Gilbert critique this position by pointing out that these assumptions are based on an individualistic binary ('right/wrong') perspective in which individuals' essentially self-interested behaviour should be curbed for the common good, rather than starting from a position which places relationship and relational contexts at the centre of deliberations. Summarising the work of Carol Gilligan (1982), Cavicchia and Gilbert state that 'a relational orientation emphasises the fundamental and inevitable interconnectedness of human beings and, therefore, makes foreground the importance of how people take into account the influences and requirements of responsibility, fairness, justice and connectedness' (2019: 206). Cavicchia and Gilbert recognise the need for guiding principles but call for a much greater emphasis on focusing on how people co-construct meaning together (notably through language and its use in particular contexts).

The issue of ethics and morality has been under consideration for many centuries. Our position is to recognise the complexity of the concept of 'being ethical' while also acknowledging the need for advanced practitioners to navigate this complexity in their coaching relationships and conversations. A leading proponent of non-directive coaching, Bob Thomson (2009), presents a pragmatic approach to ethics when he highlights the key issues for coaches:

•   the centrality of confidentiality (with the usual professional caveats)
•   boundary management (staying within the accepted definition of what constitutes coaching)
•   the voluntary engagement of the coachee with the purpose and process of the coaching (accepting that the coachee may have legitimate concerns that need to be addressed).

We believe that another pragmatic response of advanced practitioners is to sign up to the codes of ethics of their local professional associations. However, depending on the complexities involved, simply being a member of a professional association and adhering to a code of ethics may not be sufficient. Subscribing to a code of ethics and accepting the principles on which they are based does not necessarily translate into knowing how to *act* when the ethical moment of choice occurs. This is borne out by research that found a considerable degree of confusion amongst coaches about how to respond to a range of typical ethical issues (Passmore, Csigsas & Brown, 2017). In addition, de Haan's work suggests that for many coaches, 'ethics is about conformity to ethical codes. If the code says it's forbidden then it is forbidden; if the code doesn't forbid it then it is acceptable' (2012: 105). Evidently, an advanced practitioner will have a more sophisticated relationship with ethics based on their reflective practice and continuously developing ethical maturity.

De Haan suggests that there are a range of responses to an ethical moment:

- we may not recognise an ethical moment until after the event
- we may recognise it but be confused about how to proceed
- we can be clear what to do – but not follow through by doing it
- we can be clear about what not to do – and still do it
- we may know the right thing to do, take that action, yet be unable to explain our decision-making process or to justify our thinking and behaviour, including in relation to the code of ethics with which we aspire to comply. (2012: 105)

In our view, one characteristic of advanced practice is the ability of a coach to notice an ethical moment of choice, to reflect on this and take appropriate action, and then be able to justify that action based on a relevant code of ethics.

Iordanou, Hawley and Iordanou (2017) highlight the complexities of ethical decision making in coaching and compare the professional position on ethics with the prevailing conditions in the health service. They are salutary in pointing out that while NHS ethical codes are vital, their existence has not prevented some major scandals in the healthcare sector. Coaching draws on many of the principles which underpin ethical practice in health. Iordanou, Hawley and Iordanou suggest that coaches' ethical decision making relies on a combination of two sources: their own individual moral compass and the code of ethics they sign up to when they join a professional body. From the perspective of potential legal challenge, they suggest that the moral compass on its own is insufficiently robust, and the latter does not preclude the possibility of poor behaviour. They may also be too prescriptive to offer support, beyond providing simple guidance when faced with the intense complexities of some ethical matters. They also attest that 'doing the right thing' may not 'feel right' to the coach. They refer to a common scenario where as a result of a coaching conversation, the coachee decides to leave the organisation that has paid for her professional development. How does the coach decide whether her obligations to the sponsor outweigh maintaining confidentiality for her coachee? Is there a contextualised ethical 'third way' to be found?

Let us now consider the topic of personal values. Iordanou, Hawley and Iordanou define values as 'a set of personal principles that guide our behaviour and, by extension, our coaching practice' (2017: 12). They note how rapidly (or not) societal changes have shaped those personal principles in a range of important areas (e.g. same sex relationships, corporal punishment and freedom of expression). They see ethics as the 'moral principles that govern a person's behaviour or the conducting of a behaviour' (p. 16). Ethics then 'refer to a person's decisions and actions, as dictated by their beliefs and values' (p. 16). Again, historically, definitions and perspectives on ethics have shifted such that a post-modern, narrative ethics approach is based on an assertion that a universal standard code is virtually impossible and specific contextual and professional factors must be taken into account in shaping ethical thinking in different fields. Iordanou, Hawley and Iordanou conclude that 'ethical moments of choice' will arise continually in the work of coaches. They recommend that advanced practitioners should notice these moments because 'they alert us to what is morally right or wrong' (p. 25). It is particularly important to notice when coaches are concerned about a decision that they have made in their practice. According to Iordanou, Hawley and Iordanou, 'the right level of worry is indicative of your commitment to your clients ... The key to success is to maintain a conscious and recurrent ethical thinking, and to continuously reflect on your own values and how they can influence the decisions you make' (p. 25).

As we have seen in other parts of this book, the quality of the relationship between coach and coachee is receiving increasing attention in the field. Iordanou, Hawley and Iordanou underline the importance of the relationship by placing it centre-stage in the development of ethical practice. In particular they focus on:

- confidentiality and trust
- contracting – so that both coach and coachee have a clear understanding of the purpose of the coaching, and their respective roles
- coachee autonomy
- working with 'challenging' coachees – by which they mean coachees who cause us to take stock ethically
- ending the coaching relationship. (2017: 53–63)

Advanced practitioners continue to refine their coaching practice and their ethical maturity through experience and reflective practice. By doing this, advanced practitioners become familiar with their personal values and adept at working within codes of ethics. They also develop an ability to listen to themselves better.

USING OUR INTUITION

Advanced practitioners make significant use of their intuition, which Berne defines as knowing 'something without knowing how we know it' (1969, quoted in Phillips,

2006: 9). Keri Phillips describes intuition as 'a sudden insight, but without any understanding of the source' (2006: 9). The challenge, as Gary Klein points out, is that skilled decision-makers 'may feel uncomfortable trusting a source of power that seems so accidental' (1998, quoted in Phillips, 2006: 9). De Haan discusses the role of intuition in ethical decision making: 'There are convincing indications that many (if not most) decisions are made intuitively before our conscious mind notes, validates and justifies them using reason and language' (2012: 108). His conclusion is that coaches should learn to trust their intuitive responses. According to de Haan, these intuitive responses are based on experience and current practice. However, de Haan cautions that when making ethical decisions coaches should be alert to the different attributions they make about their own and others' actions and intentions (p. 108).

Daniel Kahneman (2011) considers whether we can trust 'expert intuition' and critiques the magical perception of intuitive endeavour as 'knowing without knowing'. He draws on Klein's (1998) work with firefighters to illustrate that intuitive decision making is based on a coherent process, albeit one that may be appear on the surface to have no obvious structure. Klein found that expert firefighters, rather than weighing up a range of possibilities, opted for one course of action, which they then tested against their previous experience and the prevailing circumstances. If the course of action fell short, they modified the plan. If it was deemed to be unworkable, they moved to another option and repeated the process. In explaining this intuitive process, Kahneman quotes Simon: 'The situation has provided a cue; this cue has given the expert access to information stored in memory, and the information provides the answer. Intuition is nothing more and nothing less than recognition' (Simon, quoted in Kahneman, 2011: 237). For Kahneman, there are strong elements of emotional learning involved. The feelings associated with an experience help to embed it in our memory and a repeat of the feelings in a different setting triggers a recognition of the original experience. This emotional learning can happen quickly. However, expertise in a field takes time to acquire. 'Expertise in a domain is not a single skill but rather a collection of miniskills' (Kahneman, 2011: 238). Based on a collaboration with Gary Klein, Kahneman proposes that we can trust our own (and others') intuitive responses when two foundational conditions are in place:

- an environment that is sufficiently regular to be predictable
- an opportunity to learn these regularities through prolonged practice. (Klein, 1998, in Kahneman, 2011: 240)

It can be argued that the environment in coaching is not predictable and therefore there is insufficient regularity to underpin sustained practice. Kahneman (2011) recognises the complexities involved in professional fields where 'wicked' irregular environments can lead to experts 'learning the wrong thing'. He cites the role of experts in the finance field whose intuition led them away from the clues that the system was failing and into a false confidence that everything was working well. Kahneman suggests key elements in the honing of intuitive thinking and decision making are the quality and speed of feedback and opportunities to practise.

What does all this mean for coaching? There are some resonances with Kahneman's work. At one level the environment in coaching is largely irregular given we are working with individuals who are involved in many different organisational contexts. Conversely, there are some regularities accruing from factors such as the basic features of a coaching conversation. Coaches have many opportunities to practise Kahneman's 'mini-skills', such as asking powerful questions, empathic listening, and contracting. Phillips' (2006) research into intuition in coaching suggests that intuition can be triggered when a number of conditions are in place:

- there is a creative tension between a clearly articulated future vision and a well-researched current reality
- there is time and space to reflect and explore without a 'rush to discover the truth' or the stringency of adhering to a particular coaching method (p. 30)
- coach and coachee are open to the potential of intuition, embrace confusion and 'half-grasped truths' (p. 48), and balance seriousness and playfulness
- the coachee is curious about herself, without being self-obsessed.

Advanced practitioners should therefore be continually learning. In this way they are developing their intuition so that they are better able to respond effectively to their coachees' needs and any ethical moments of choice that may emerge.

POWER IN COACHING RELATIONSHIPS

Given that coaching is meant to be facilitative, open and strongly client-focused, it is easy to be lulled into thinking that power dynamics are absent from coaching relationships. However, coaches have the potential of significant levels of power over coachees derived from a number of sources. To use French and Raven's (1959) terms, coaches have 'expert power' based on their distinctive knowledge and skills related to coaching processes. A coachee may admire her coach for her expertise in enabling her to work constructively through complex scenarios, and this can create power over the coachee which advanced practitioners must use ethically. At a more 'in-the-moment' level, every question the coach asks, however exploratory and open, closes down other lines of inquiry. This gives the advanced practitioner power over the direction of a conversation, which again should be used sensitively and ethically.

Referring back to French and Raven's taxonomy (1959), it becomes apparent that coaches may also have power as a result of the information held about the coachee, her context and her sponsors' intentions and goals. There may be times, particularly in the initial stages of establishing the contract with the sponsor, when the coach may be privy to information that is not available to the coachee. Further, the coachee may also perceive that the coach has 'reward power' based on an actual or presumed ability to bring about positive consequences. 'Legitimate power' may also be a factor if the sponsor has commissioned the coach and she is seen as having organisational authority. The one source of power that is usually less present is 'coercive power' (the perceived ability to punish others in some way). These sources of power will be thrown into stark relief if a coach challenges a coachee about a decision that raises ethical questions.

Above, we have briefly considered the issue of perceived power of the coach over the coachee. Clearly, there is also the possibility that the coachee holds power over the coach. For example, the coachee may deploy her particular professional expertise in ways that undermine the coach's confidence and ability to use trusted methods. The coachee's role may also seem to place them 'above' the coach in the work hierarchy, especially where the coachee is a chief executive and the coach has not held such a role. When the coachee pays for the coaching herself, this positions the coach as a contractor or employee, giving the coachee power in the relationship. All of these potential sources of power are also affected significantly by the dynamics pertaining in wider society. Class, gender, race, sexual orientation and identity, and political perspective will also be factors affecting the building and sustaining of successful, equitable coaching relationships.

PUTTING IT INTO PRACTICE

In our experience, novice coaches tend to approach ethics with a desire to find 'right or wrong' answers. They may be confused and concerned about the *right* ethical approach to those issues and appropriately turn to the professional codes of practice for guidance. However, while those essential codes provide a helpful backdrop to ethical decision making, they cannot provide absolute answers for challenges that are highly contextual. As a result, novice coaches can be anxious about coming face to face with ethical issues. Advanced practitioners with more experience of managing ethical moments of choice will recognise and acknowledge the ambiguities inherent in ethical challenges and are likely to see them as situations requiring careful management in order to balance the differential impacts of possible courses of action.

Therefore, it is important for advanced practitioners to develop what a number of writers in the field refer to as 'ethical maturity'. In summary, this involves:

- being actively alert to ethical sensitivities and seeking out 'ethical moments of choice', embracing them positively as a means of surfacing matters that are important to achieving the desired outcomes of the coaching
- noticing in the moment when they are feeling uncertain, concerned or challenged by something in the coaching conversation
- taking a relational perspective that positions the moment of choice as an opportunity to test and strengthen the relationship with her coachee
- adopting a systemic perspective that acknowledges and explores factors around and beyond the coaching relationship in the service of her coachee
- judging that the relationship is sufficiently robust and trusting to enable sensitive or difficult feedback to be given to her coachee
- taking calculated risks that challenging her coachee will not, in the long run, undermine or damage the coaching relationship
- being open and clear, at appropriate moments, about her own values and ethical stance in order to stimulate reflection and reflexivity in her coachee
- maintaining a high level of self-confidence in her abilities and experience, trusting that these will be impactful in enabling her coachee to gain insights later on
- facilitating the conversation so that the coachee can uncover, deconstruct and reconstruct the prevailing narratives and their associated language to come to a clearer understanding of the meaning that she and significant others are making of the topic of focus.

The advanced practitioner is comfortable with the notion that there are no absolutes in ethical decision making and that there will be upsides and downsides to any course of action, which will require further reflection and action as part of any resolution. She checks her assumptions and triangulates her responses through self-reflection and reflexivity after every session, keeping detailed journals about her thinking, and exploring ethical moments of choice with peers and her supervisor. Crucially, she sees encounters with ethical moments of choice not just as opportunities for her coachee to learn and develop, but as important staging posts in her own continuing growth as a coach.

This approach to ethical moments of choice needs to be balanced with a confident approach to a coach's personal values. The challenge that arises is how advanced practitioners live according to their values while not dominating or imposing them on their coachees. Advanced practitioners therefore need to be clear in their continuous contracting how their values will affect their work and the specifics of each relationship with their coachees, declaring sensitively where they might be coming from in relation to wider social outcomes. This will require high degrees of self-awareness and emotional intelligence, consummate skill in the exploration of sensitive matters in ways that complement rather than overpower the coachee's agenda, and the courage to be relentlessly determined to make a difference for the coachee, her organisation and the wider system.

8
BEING WHO YOU ARE AND ADAPTING TO OTHERS

Stories from our practice: Identifying with the coachee

In one coaching assignment, I worked with a senior leader in the public sector who was grappling with the implications of budget cuts. 'Ahmed' entered public service many years ago with the intention of making a difference to people's lives. At this point in his career, he believed that his decisions were about to have a significant and detrimental impact on service provision. Making the best use of his organisation's scarce resources, Ahmed was trying to do the best job he could so that he might mitigate the worst effects of financial cutbacks on his local community.

During this session, I found myself identifying with Ahmed's predicament. Before becoming a coach, I too had worked for many years in public services. I remembered that I also had to make difficult resource allocation decisions, even though these were in earlier times before the climate of austerity took hold. I hold similar values to Ahmed and I could relate to the pressures and dilemma he was facing. I've always had a strong interest in politics and in my younger days was active in campaigns to save local public services. While I appreciate and support the need for public services to make efficient use of public money and to adopt a continuous improvement approach to provision, I believe they need to be 'business-like' rather than run like private businesses. I find the current cutbacks in public service provision difficult to accept and believe that austerity is being driven by ideology and not the real needs of people.

All of these reflections were active for me during the coaching conversation. I noticed that Ahmed's predicament was causing him considerable consternation, bordering on physical pain. I noticed that I started to feel an ache in my chest and stomach. This

(Continued)

(Continued)

reminded me of the observation of the poet David Whyte on pain: 'Pain is the first proper step to real compassion; it can be a foundation for understanding all those who struggle with their existence. Experiencing real pain ourselves, our moral superiority comes to an end; we stop urging others to get with the programme, to get their act together or to sharpen up ... In pain we suddenly find our understanding and compassion engaged as to why others may find it hard to fully participate' (2015).

I have friends who experience the fallout of decisions like those Ahmed faces. The impacts on them come in the form of the withdrawal of a service, poorer quality provision or increasing difficulties in 'proving' they are still 'deserving' of the services they rely on. I know I am the kind of coach who works most effectively when I bring myself fully to coaching relationships. How can I be authentic in working with Ahmed?

Traditional notions of coaching would suggest that I should remind myself that my role is to support Ahmed do his job well and work towards the best decision that achieves his organisation's objectives, while taking account of the impact on services. However, this approach, while pragmatic, feels to me an inadequate response to the emotions initiated by the conflict with Ahmed's values. I was left with a number of burning questions:

- How would being more open about my values and true reactions help Ahmed?
- How can I constructively use the feeling that I might be colluding with 'the system' by helping Ahmed make decisions that I know will impact negatively on people's lives?
- What will be the impact on our relationship, and the trust, integrity and honesty on which it is based, if Ahmed does *not* get some sense of my response to his intense emotions?
- *How much* authenticity is helpful in this relationship?

A widely accepted tenet of coaching places the coachee at the centre of the coach's focus of attention. As coaching has developed, there has been increasing interest in the authenticity of the coach. A particularly pertinent question is the extent to which a coach should bring her 'true self' to coaching sessions. If coaches are to be *themselves* in coaching conversations, how does this influence the requirement to adapt their approaches to meet the needs and interests of their coachees? How does being 'who you are as a coach' enable practitioners to be flexible and responsive to the myriad diverse facets of humanity that they are sure to encounter in their practice?

A seminal text about education advises its readers to 'be yourself – don't feel being a teacher means you have to behave like a "teacher". As far as possible speak in ways you normally speak, respond as yourself rather than as you think a "teacher" should respond. Students ... very quickly see through someone who is role-playing what they think a teacher should be. Authenticity in you tends to draw the best out of those you are working with' (Scrivener, 2005: 36). While these reflections are about teachers, the ideas resonate with coaches too. In this chapter, we will explore what 'bringing yourself' to coaching might feel like in practice. We will draw on writing and thinking in the coaching and leadership development fields.

PERSPECTIVES ON 'AUTHENTICITY'

The authenticity of leaders has received significant attention in the field of professional development. For example, the Virtual Staff College (VSC) highlighted the importance of a leader's 'way of being' which 'forms the essence of both professional and personal style and approach' (Ghate, Lewis and Welbourn, 2013: 6). This way of being is seen as providing an overarching framework for other vital system leadership qualities such as personal core values (ways of feeling), observations and perceptions (ways of perceiving), cognition, analysis and synthesis (ways of thinking), participatory style (ways of relating), and behaviours and actions (ways of doing). Blyth, Olson and Walker (2017) similarly highlight the importance of social and emotional learning for the holistic education of young people. Critiquing an over-emphasis on 'ways of doing' in education, they suggest that ways of feeling and relating are the means by which decisions about actions (the 'doing') are appropriately contextualised in order to identify ways to approach tasks and achieve goals.

Leadership writers Werner Erhard and Michael Jensen (2014) identify four 'ways of being' that form the foundation of effective leadership:

- Being authentic – 'being and acting consistently with who you hold yourself out to be for others, and who you hold yourself to be for yourself'. (2014: 3)
- Being cause in the matter of everything in your life – this is the 'stand you take on yourself and your life. A stand is a declaration you make, not a statement of fact' and forms the basis for how one's life is viewed. (2014: 6)
- Being committed to something bigger than oneself – this refers to 'being committed in a way that shapes one's being and actions so that your ways of being and acting are in the service of realizing something beyond your personal concerns for yourself'. (2014: 7)
- Being a person of integrity – integrity means a person's word being 'whole and complete' and is vital for creating opportunities to generate trust. (2014: 7)

Erhard and Jensen (2014) emphasise that their framework is not focused on a particular, specified set of values and advocate that these four foundations are in every individual's self-interest, regardless of the values they hold. For them, being truly authentic involves being authentic about the times and circumstances when we are *inauthentic*. This suggests that the coach should notice when she is being less authentic and, crucially, know *why* she is choosing not to be fully authentic in the circumstances.

Executive coaches Graham Lee and Ian Roberts explain that authentic leadership 'emphasises the paradoxical nature of leadership; it contains not only the personal authenticity of leaders being true to themselves, accurately representing their intentions and commitments with emotional genuineness but also the "social authenticity" of being true to the needs of the situation, attuned to others and the context, and to the impact the leaders are likely to have on others. Leadership is what is co-created between the leader and the led' (2010: 18). They make a distinction between authentic leadership, where character strengths and organisational goals are creatively attuned, and 'compliant' and 'defiant' leadership. Compliant leaders are 'other-focused' and have limited spontaneity, while defiant leaders are self-focused with limited attunement to others. Lee and Roberts highlight the importance of leaders being reflectively aware (p. 21). They also propose that coaches should be role models of 'reflective awareness' with a clear understanding of their own particular biases towards compliance and defiance and how these can impede bringing out the best in others (p. 29). Leadership coach Doug MacKie (2016) argues that the concept of authentic leadership emerged as a way of distinguishing genuine transformational leaders from manipulative ones. He refers to the work of Walumbwa (2008), who identifies four key constructs underpinning authentic leadership:

- balanced processing in decision making
- an internalised moral perspective
- relational transparency with others
- self-awareness. (in MacKie, 2016: 51)

Leading educational thinker Michael Fullan takes this further, placing clear 'moral purpose' as a central attribute of effective leaders of change (2004: 13).

While there has been considerable enthusiasm for the concept of authentic leadership, it is important to acknowledge that some are sceptical about the concept. For example, Tourish sees authentic leadership as having similarities to the more traditional 'heroic' leadership paradigm in the 'over-attribution of agency' to leaders and in playing down the need to use coercion to overcome non-conforming behaviours (2013, in MacKie 2016: 184). One of the critiques of the authentic leadership approach is the problematic dynamic of the fact that the dominant values are primarily those of the leader, rather than being co-created with those they lead. This is likely to lead to insufficient recognition and appreciation of the wider context and culture of the organisation or society.

MacKie proposes another critique with an intriguing question: Is it possible for leaders to have 'too much authenticity'? (2016: 52). For example, too much self-confidence might tip over into arrogance, which will have a negative influence on a leader's relationship with her followers. He also questions what it means to be authentic in a period of austerity. If leaders are attempting to work to a set of values that are in conflict with the direction of change, how can they remain true to themselves? Acknowledging power differences in organisations, MacKie points to leaders 'who are understandably cautious of speaking openly and directly in a climate of efficiency drives, cost reduction and capital restraint' (p. 52). This is something that we have encountered in our own practice. As demonstrated in the 'Story from our practice' at the start of this chapter, coachees can often find themselves feeling challenged by the mismatch between the values that drew them into their roles and the leadership behaviours that might be expected by their organisations.

In *Diversity in Coaching* (2009), Tinu Cornish reports on a study of successful women leaders from BAME (Black, Asian and Minority Ethnic) backgrounds. The study identified eight core leadership qualities that contributed to their success and were influenced by their experience as BAME women:

- 'Bicultural competence – being familiar with both British values and the norms of their ethnic group gave them the ability to lead across cultures.
- Multiple perspectives – cultural breadth and learning from the challenges faced because of their race and gender gave them the ability to see things from multiple perspectives and often come up with novel solutions to problems.
- Cultural capital – experience gained outside the workplace built their leadership and motivational skills.
- Transformational leadership – being able to challenge the status quo and implement change plus transactional skills ... regularly delivering results.
- Self-mastery – a sense of assuredness in their innate talents and a resilience to deal with challenges and setbacks.
- Presence, passion and power – able to communicate their views with conviction and enthusiasm and hold the attention of others.
- Value-driven leadership – being guided primarily by a desire to make a positive contribution to their organisations and communities.
- Spiritual belief – in no small way fundamental to their success'. (2009: 172)

Cornish points out that these qualities are 'very similar to those thought to be essential for authentic leaders' (2009: 172). Authentic leaders establish long-term meaningful relationships and have the self-discipline to get results. They know who they are and typically report that overcoming difficult challenges in their lives was the catalyst for developing a passion to lead.

Taking a slightly different approach, leadership consultant and author Peter Block sees authenticity as involving learning 'how to develop ... inner strength and to help others learn it' (2001: 157). For him, a crucial element is the exploration of anxiety as a means of generating strength: 'Anxiety, far from being a sickness, is the actual experience of being strong, of growing, of building character, of achieving pride. Anxiety is how it feels to grow authentically into the human being we were meant to be' (p. 157). One aspect of advanced practice relates to the way in which coaches encounter and respond to anxiety and frustration. Taking into account that many coaching conversations revolve around the 'stuckness' of the coachee, these strong feelings are likely to be experienced. Advanced practitioners are therefore able to recognise, value and harness the anxiety and frustration that they notice in their clients. At the same time, advanced practitioners notice and manage situations when they experience anxiety or frustration during a coaching conversation.

ANXIETY AND FRUSTRATION

Coaching conversations are an opportunity for people to work towards a desired future state in the presence of a coach. Coaching is understood to be a helpful conversation that will make it more likely that goals are achieved, or desired outcomes attained. Based on this perspective, coachees seek out coaching because they believe that it will facilitate or expedite the achievement of goals that may be challenging to achieve. Often, the coachee doubts her own ability to achieve a desired outcome. At other times, she is trying to understand what is holding her back. Almost always there is a feeling of 'being stuck' or of 'not knowing'. 'Being stuck' is likely to cause varying levels of frustration (from mild annoyance through to anger) and 'not knowing' is likely to cause varying levels of anxiety (from nervousness through to fear).

When novice coaches are faced with strong feelings, there is a tendency to try to minimise these or avoid the topics that cause these feelings. In fact, it would be quite authentic to want to talk about something else. In other words, if a person is experiencing painful emotions, a typical response would be to reassure the person experiencing painful emotions and show sympathy. Further, novice coaches are more likely to be overwhelmed by the strong emotions of their coachees, leading to changes in their coaching approach and behaviours. Initially, when faced with coachees who are expressing anger or fear, many coaches may feel ill-equipped to manage these strong feelings. A consequence can be for novice coaches to downplay the emotions or avoid the topic causing the strong feelings.

Focus on practice: Responding to anxiety and frustration

What is different between the way that a novice coach and an advanced practitioner may encounter the same strong emotions with authenticity? The first is the stance that the advanced practitioner takes. The second is that the advanced practitioner follows an intentional process.

Stance

Over time, and with reflexivity, it is possible for advanced practitioners to develop a positive stance towards experiences of frustration or anxiety that will influence the coaching interaction. Advanced practitioners will recognise that both frustration and anxiety can be used positively. Frustration is a response to perceived resistance or obstacles that prevent an individual from achieving her goals or intentions. Because it is a natural response to feeling 'stuck', it is a useful emotion when supporting coachees to overcome obstacles or tackle the resistance that is preventing them from achieving their goals. In other words, when a coachee reports feeling frustrated, or the advanced practitioner senses frustration during the session, this is an indication that the coachee is motivated to change the status quo. The dissatisfaction with the current situation can be harnessed to drive new thinking and behaviours in order to overcome the perceived barriers, challenges and resistance. Similarly, anxiety is a normal response to stressful situations. Often, anxiety is the natural reaction to perceived threats. So, anxiety experienced during a coaching conversation can indicate a strong negative reaction to the current situation or worry about an imagined future step that may be required to move closer to the coachee's goal. An advanced practitioner is likely to notice frustration and anxiety during coaching conversations and respond positively, treating the emotions as useful information about the coachee's current level of readiness for change.

Advanced practitioners who have adopted this stance are likely to follow a process, even if this is not explicit. We will discuss one process that can be used for the sake of elaborating further on this thinking. The important element of advanced practice is taking the stance above, not following a specific process. Each advanced practitioner will have her own preferred ways of harnessing frustration and anxiety.

Process

- Creating safety in the partnership and developing a positive relationship.
- Noticing frustration or anxiety in the moment.
- Determining the source of the frustration or anxiety.
- Managing and bracketing one's own sense of frustration or anxiety.
- Raising awareness of the sense of frustration or anxiety.
- Using this awareness to gain commitment to an alternative future.

Creating safety in the partnership and developing a positive relationship

Creating a safe space is a fundamental aspect of all coaching conversations, and therefore not specific to advanced practice. It is a core skill of being a coach. Without safety and a positive relationship, advanced practitioners are likely to miss out on important information about their coachees.

(Continued)

(Continued)

Noticing frustration or anxiety in the moment

This is about *noticing* frustration or anxiety from a position of professional detachment, not only *experiencing* these emotions. The advanced practitioner will be alert for indications of frustration (such as irritation, boredom and impatience) and anxiety (such as nervous energy, unease and catastrophising).

Determining the source of the frustration or anxiety

The advanced practitioner tries to determine the source of any frustration or anxiety that is noticed. When the advanced practitioner notices 'anxiety', for example, has this come to her awareness because *she* is experiencing anxiety in relation to her own role as coach? This kind of anxiety is both legitimate and common – in both novice and experienced coaches. However, advanced practitioners have the self-awareness and honesty to acknowledge that the anxiety has been generated from their own self-doubt or concerns.

Managing and bracketing one's own sense of frustration or anxiety

The advanced practitioner will be able to distinguish between anxiety that emerges from the conversation, the relationship or the coachee, and anxiety that is primarily generated by the coach herself. Anxiety generated by the coach will need to be bracketed (noticed, acknowledged and earmarked for later consideration) and then taken into reflective practice or supervision.

Raising awareness of the sense of frustration or anxiety

Advanced practitioners, in being authentic and focused on the best interests of their coachees, will be able to raise awareness about the frustration or anxiety during the coaching conversation. Advanced practitioners will undertake this tentatively and with compassion, taking ownership for what has been noticed and shared. It is sufficient to raise awareness of frustration or anxiety without any immediate pressure to resolve the issues that have caused the emotions.

Using this awareness to gain commitment to an alternative future

The raised awareness of the frustration or anxiety (in the coach or the coachee) can then be identified as a driver for thinking and talking together about a preferred, alternative future. Frustration and anxiety are therefore used positively by the advanced practitioner to create added urgency for moving forward.

Focus on practice: Ontological coaching

Ontological coaching provides a way of addressing authenticity and coaches' responses. Ontology is the study of 'being' and human existence. Alan Sieler (2018) describes the dynamic interplay between the three domains (language, emotions and body) as the 'way of being'. For him 'the essential goal of the coach is to be a catalyst for change by respectfully and constructively perturbing the coachee to enable him or her to self-generate constructive new perceptions and behaviours that are consistent with what the coachee wants to gain from coaching' (p. 97). It follows that the coach's responsibility is to manage her own way of being in the coaching conversation. Sieler asserts that the only place coaches can coach from 'is their own way of being, which will affect how (i) acutely they observe the specifics of the coachee's way of being and (ii) they facilitate potential shifts in the coachee's way of being' (p. 93). This means that it is the role of advanced practitioners to create safe spaces for exploration within mutually respectful relationships.

SELF-AWARENESS AND REFLECTION

Another critique of the concept of authentic leadership is that there seems to be a presupposition that leaders have a good sense of 'who they really are'. This is not necessarily the case, and the pursuit of self-discovery has a long history, particularly in the fields of spirituality and religion, and many have persevered for years in search of self-enlightenment. In his book *The Power of Now* (2011), Eckhart Tolle invites us to focus less on 'doing' and more on 'being'. 'Who you are is always a more vital teaching and a more powerful transformer of the world than what you say, or more essential even than what you do' (p. 167). Tolle encourages the removal of 'ego' from the equation. He suggests that people tend to derive their sense of self from thinking, which fuels the ego. Tolle sees ego as the 'false self' (p. 18), which is preoccupied with the past and the future, ignoring the here and now despite the fact that 'nothing exists outside the now' (p. 41). We have already explored the need for advanced practitioners to be fully present in the moment (Chapter 4: Being fully present and attending to the wider context). Additionally, advanced practitioners should have a wide repertoire of coaching approaches that go beyond those that simply emphasise thinking, talking and doing. In Tolle's words, 'when listening to another person, don't just listen with your mind, listen with your whole body' (p. 105).

Eunice Aquilina agrees that authenticity is 'not a destination, or something we put on, but an on-going inquiry into the self we are and how we live our lives as a full expression of our values and beliefs' (2016: 197). She goes on to argue that coaches should pay attention to whether the actions they take are aligned with their idea of why they exist on the planet. According to Aquilina, it is through practice that we develop an 'integrated way of being, where there is no separation between our inner world and our outer world' (p. 197). This is a helpful reminder of the critical importance of reflexivity for the advanced practitioner.

Focus on practice: Being who you are and responding to the needs of others

As we reflect on the need for advanced practitioners to strive towards authenticity while also being responsive to the needs of their coachees, a few key messages seem to be emerging.

Authenticity is an integral part of a 'coaching way of being'

Authenticity seems to be an integral part of a way of being. An advanced practitioner is highly self-aware and this awareness should include clarity about her strengths and limitations, and the values that underpin her motivation and actions. She reflects on her purpose which connects with a bigger picture of the world, through which she demonstrates and communicates her passion for the work she does.

Authenticity requires the management of emotions and behaviours

Advanced practitioners are able to manage their emotions and behaviours appropriately in order to be effective with others. Ways of feeling and ways of relating provide firm foundations for 'the doing'.

To be authentic, it is necessary to be honest and open

Advanced practitioners are comfortable with being open and honest. This supports the need for coaches to operate with integrity. At times, advanced practitioners will need to reflect on whether or not to disclose certain thoughts or emotions to their coachees, and this will need to be based on their coachees' best interests.

MANAGING AUTHENTICITY AND ADVANCED PRACTICE

While personal authenticity (or being who you are) is important, the impact of this on the coaching relationship is just as crucial. Being personally authentic should not be detrimental to the best interests of coachees. As we have seen with authentic leadership, paying too much attention to being authentic might risk shifting attention away from others and more towards oneself. In coaching, this might be experienced by the coachee as too much self-disclosure by the coach. While this chapter may have implied that being a good coach is 'all about who you are', when an advanced practitioner is having a coaching conversation it should feel like it's all about the *coachee*. The challenge is that this is not easy to achieve. Some coaches refer to themselves as 'catalysts' for the learning and development of others. In scientific terms, catalysts are chemicals that enable reactions to take place while emerging from the process unchanged. This is not the case in coaching, nor do we want it to be. Advanced practitioners are *part of* the conversation and are always changing and in the process of becoming while they work with coachees who are similarly growing and developing.

Effective novice coaches understand well that the focus in coaching needs to be on the coachee. They are able to use coaching methods competently and through such processes enable coachees to gain valuable insights. This is the baseline for doing a good job as a coach. Without detracting from the ability of these coaches to deploy coaching methods, it might be argued that simple yet sophisticated frameworks like GROW (Whitmore, 2009) have, by design, an in-built potential for success. GROW, for example, exists as a much-used problem-solving process beyond the boundaries of coaching. Overly focusing on process might mean that insights are more likely to be stumbled across, rather than emerging from a deeper connection between coach and coachee, increasing the chances of the coaching conversation moving beyond the transactional into an experience for the coachee that is truly transformational. Advanced practitioners are adept at using a range of coaching approaches too. By paying attention to 'how they turn up' and what they personally bring to the table, advanced practitioners deploy their authenticity in the service of their coachees.

9
BEING COMMITTED TO OUTCOMES AND PRIORITISING WELLBEING

Visit https://study.sagepub.com/advancedcoaching to watch the video discussed in this chapter:

VIDEO 9.1: Paying attention to the wellbeing of the coachee

The remarkable growth of the executive coaching industry has been driven largely by the promise of improved performance at work. In other words, many people seek out coaching as a way of enhancing individual, group, team and organisational performance. This tendency is encouraged by executive coaching providers, coach training organisations and the professional associations that have emerged over the last 20 years.

The origin of the concept of 'coaching for performance' can be traced directly back to one of the leading figures in the field of executive coaching, Sir John Whitmore. He successfully promoted the notion of coaching for performance by exploring how concepts derived from competitive sports might be relevant in corporate contexts. In fact, Whitmore's seminal text, *Coaching for Performance*, is the field's best-selling book. Now in its fifth edition (2017), it makes a strong case for the use of coaching to enhance the *performance* of coachees. In his introduction to the fourth edition (2009), Whitmore explained that when he wrote the first edition in 1992, 'there were hardly any other books on new coaching methods for applications beyond sport. My purpose was to define and establish the root principles of coaching before too many people jumped on the fledgling coaching bandwagon, some of whom might not have fully understood the psychological depth and potential breadth of coaching, and where it fits in the wider social context' (Whitmore, 2009: 1). Notably, Whitmore emphasises that 'the objective of improving performance is paramount' (p. 9), claiming that coaching is 'the essential management style or tool for optimizing people's potential and performance' (p. 95). Much more recently, Tatiana Bachkirova, Elaine Cox and David Clutterbuck define coaching as a 'human development process that involves structured, focused interaction and the use of appropriate strategies, tools and techniques to promote desirable and sustainable change for the benefit of the coachee and potentially for other stakeholders' (2014: 1). This focus on performance characterises the stance of many executive coaches in the field today. Indeed, this attention on the ability of coaches to bring about behavioural change seems to drive the commercial success of business, executive and performance coaching.

While this focus on performance or behavioural change is welcome and appropriate, it is important at this point to sound a note of caution. None of the early proponents of coaching was advocating performance enhancement or behavioural change *at all costs*. The wellbeing of coachees is a primary concern from the outset, and this is either implicit or explicit in early definitions. For example, Jenny Rogers proposes that coaching has multiple aims. According to her, 'coaching is the art of facilitating another person's learning, development, *well-being* and performance' [our emphasis] (2016: 7). Coaching has, as one of its objectives, the facilitation of a coachee's wellbeing. Carol Wilson, another key figure in the field, is explicit about this too. For her, coaching is about 'improving the performance *and wellbeing*' [our emphasis] of coachees (2014: 11). This parallel focus on performance and wellbeing is a common theme in early definitions. Even in *Coaching for Performance*, Whitmore characterises coaching as the most effective way of producing 'sustainable optimum performance' (2009: 95). This implies that coaching can support high levels of performance that are sustainable over time – in other words, performance that does not damage the wellbeing of individuals. Sometimes, this nuanced view of the purposes of coaching (improving performance *and wellbeing*) can be lost in short coach training programmes. Indeed, some training providers may even explicitly promote the idea that coaching is *all about performance*. This is untrue and to present coaching in this way for commercial purposes is ethically questionable. Coaching is, first and foremost, a supportive human interaction. The parallel objectives of performance and wellbeing may also be lost when coach training is rolled out to managers or human resources personnel within large organisations. When these practices have to be developed across hundreds of people in multiple locations and various cultural contexts, crucial nuances can get lost in the process. When coaching is focused narrowly on improved *performance*, measurable *outcomes* or the *impact* of coaching on the bottom line, there is a considerable risk that the wellbeing of coachees will be overlooked.

Video 9.1

See it in practice: Paying attention to the wellbeing of the coachee

In this video, Bob demonstrates an interest in the coachee's wellbeing by reassuring her that her feelings about impostor syndrome are experienced by many others.

THE CONTRIBUTION OF POSITIVE PSYCHOLOGY

When arguing for the importance of wellbeing, it is helpful to turn to the emerging positive psychology movement for relevant theories, research and evidence. Positive psychology is defined as the 'scientific study of optimal human functioning [that] aims to discover and promote the factors that allow individuals and communities to thrive' (Seligman & Csikszentmihalyi, 2000). In other words, positive psychology is the scientific study of what Whitmore identified as the purpose of coaching: 'sustainable optimum performance' (2009: 95). It has been proposed that positive psychology and coaching have a 'shared interest in human potential, growth and wellbeing' (van Nieuwerburgh, Lomas & Burke, 2018: 99). Both fields seek to increase human flourishing. One of the founders of positive psychology, Chris Peterson, explained it in this way: 'What is good about life is as genuine as what is bad and therefore deserves equal attention from psychologists. It assumes that life entails more than avoiding or undoing problems and hassles. Positive psychology resides some-where in that part of the human landscape that is metaphorically north of neutral. It is the study of what we are doing when we are not frittering life away' (2006: 4).

One of the areas of study within positive psychology is 'subjective wellbeing'. Positive psychologists are 'intrigued by the potential benefits that positive emotions, and 'positiv-ity' more broadly (encompassing emotions, thoughts, and behaviors), have to offer employees and organizations' (Green, McQuaid, Purtell & Dulagil, 2017: 11). The field is increasingly turning its attention to subjective wellbeing and optimal human functioning in the workplace. On the whole, when positive psychologists consider the role of indi-viduals within organisations, they tend to be committed to their performance *and wellbeing*; on their strengths rather than their weaknesses; and on human flourishing rather than languishing.

From a positive psychology perspective, a person's subjective wellbeing is enhanced when she experiences 'many positive and few negative emotions and moods, while also reporting high life and domain-specific evaluations' (Miao, Koo and Oishi, 2013: 174). Based on this theory, subjective wellbeing comprises two main components: affective wellbeing, which relates to a person's emotions; and cognitive wellbeing, which relates to how a person thinks. Cognitive wellbeing is measured by asking a person to evaluate her life. So, if a person experiences more positive emotions and fewer negative emotions, and she is satisfied with her life, this would be an indication that her subjective wellbeing is high. Alternatively, a person who experiences more negative emotions and fewer positive emotions, and is dissatisfied with her life, would be said to have low subjective wellbeing. Positive psychology is therefore interested in ways of increasing positive emotions, decreasing negative emotions and helping people to evaluate their lives more positively. Positive psychology interventions (PPIs) are designed to do this and will be discussed later in this chapter.

PRIORITISING WELLBEING

There are a number of reasons that coaches should be interested in the subjective wellbeing of their coachees. First, the ethical codes of all of the professional associations of coaching expect their members to have a duty of care towards their coachees. Second, coaches should be able to demonstrate that they have the best interests of their coachees at heart. Third, we propose that advanced practitioners are ideally placed to ensure that progress towards goals does not negatively impact on the long-term wellbeing of coachees and those around them. In this chapter, we propose that advanced practitioners should consistently *prioritise* the wellbeing of their coachees. This is especially relevant when those coachees may seem determined to achieve their self-selected goals at any cost. In this situation, there is an increased risk that coachees can lose sight of the importance of their wellbeing and those around them as they become completely committed to actions aimed at achieving important goals in their lives. Alternatively, it can be the professional context that encourages an unwavering dedication to goal attainment and performance improvement.

It may sound incongruous to propose that coaches should be overtly attentive to the wellbeing of coachees even when this is not raised as a concern by them. Some may argue that it is the responsibility of the coachees themselves to consider their own wellbeing. Further, the intention of coaches could be questioned and the focus on wellbeing could be interpreted as overly parental or nurturing. After all, would it not be judgemental of a coach to make assumptions about the wellbeing of her coachee? And what gives a coach the right to interfere in the personal lives of her coachees? Our position is that advanced practitioners should support their coachees towards *optimal performance*. We understand this to mean consistent levels of high performance that can be sustained over time. Ideally, advanced practitioners will be working with their coachees to help them achieve their desired outcomes in ways that *enhance* their physical and psychological wellbeing. In the section below, we will consider relevant positive psychology theories and share ideas about practical ways of addressing the wellbeing of coachees while supporting them to achieve meaningful goals.

Stories from our practice: Personal and professional cost

One of us took an interesting and slightly unexpected topic to our coach supervisor. The meeting was a scheduled supervision session and took place at the British Library.

I had not had much time to prepare for the coaching supervision session but was still looking forward to the conversation. As I was walking to the British Library in the afternoon drizzle, I wondered what I would bring to the conversation. The previous session had been very useful, but that topic was resolved for now. It would be most appropriate to talk about a six-session coaching contract that had recently concluded. Both the coachee and I felt very positive about the outcome of the coaching conversations. Maybe it had been so successful that there was nothing to bring to supervision. When teaching others how to coach, I often say that they should bring positive experiences to coaching supervision too – not just negative ones. So perhaps this was the opportunity to do just that. What aspect could I explore? I remembered a slight discomfort that I had experienced in the concluding conversation – it was fleeting, but it was something that might be worth discussing further. I was at the British Library now, so this would be the topic.

My supervisor was there before me and had some tea already. I ordered myself a cup of tea and joined her. After the pleasantries, she asked what I would like to explore in our conversation. I hesitated before saying, 'Yes, I'd like to talk about a coaching contract that concluded recently.' My coach supervisor encouraged me to say more. 'I'm not sure how significant this is. It was only fleeting, but I have a sense that I'd like to explore it further if that's OK with you.' She nodded. 'Well, it was a very successful series of coaching conversations, from one point of view. My client achieved almost exactly the very clear goal that we had agreed during our first meeting months ago. We had made steady progress throughout our conversations. And, just before the sixth conversation, the coachee got to where they had wanted to be. He said, "I can't believe it. It's been hard work, but I've achieved that goal that we agreed together at the very start".' My coaching supervisor nodded. 'But I had this fleeting doubt – a question – as my client thanked me for helping him to achieve his goal.' 'What was the doubt?' my supervisor asked. 'It was just the question of whether it was worth it,' I admitted. 'There was no doubt that the initial goal had been achieved, but I had been a witness to the personal and professional cost to my client of his success. When I had reflected on his achievement, the positive outcome seemed to have come at a very high cost. I guess my doubt came from that question – was it worth it? My client was so completely focused on the goal that he seemed willing to do anything to achieve it – and the reason I'm bringing this to our supervision session is that I'm worried that I encouraged him to do that.'

USING POSITIVE PSYCHOLOGY THEORIES TO PRIORITISE THE WELLBEING OF COACHEES

In this section, we will consider self-determination theory (SDT) (Ryan & Deci, 2000), the PERMA model (Seligman, 2011), broaden-and-build theory (Fredrickson, 2001), and the universal elements of wellbeing (Rath & Harter, 2010) and how they might inform advanced practice.

Self-determination theory

In their research into SDT, Richard Ryan and Edward Deci define wellbeing as 'optimal experience and functioning' (2000: 141). Based on their research, they make a convincing case that human beings must satisfy three basic psychological needs: autonomy, competence and relatedness. Therefore, if a person has a sense of autonomy, believes that she is competent in one of her primary roles and feels connected to others, SDT would suggest that she will be more likely to thrive. This means that advanced practitioners should pay attention to these three elements.

Focus on practice: Self-determination theory

During coaching conversations, SDT suggests that advanced practitioners should ensure their clients experience the three components. Below we consider ways that coaches might address autonomy, competence and relatedness.

Autonomy

- Coaches can ascertain that the goals presented by the coachee are self-selected.
- If the coachee's goals are not self-selected, it may be helpful to explore ways of embracing an externally selected goal by making it meaningful to the coachee.
- Coaches can ensure that the coachee makes most of the decisions during a coaching conversation.

Competence

- It may be helpful to remind the coachee of previous successes.
- Coaches can support their coachees to set achievable tasks between coaching sessions.
- Coaches may occasionally highlight progress that is being made towards important goals.

Relatedness

- Coaches can encourage their coachees to connect to existing personal and professional networks.
- It can be helpful to explicitly highlight the value and strength of the professional coaching relationship that has been developed between the coach and the coachee.
- Asking the coachee to explain the relationships that may need to be activated in order to achieve her goal can lead to greater appreciation of their importance.

PERMA

In a seminal positive psychology text, *Flourish*, Martin Seligman presents a model of wellbeing called PERMA (2011). This theory proposes that there are five core elements underpinning human wellbeing. According to Seligman, people can attain subjective wellbeing (and therefore flourish) if they work towards each of the elements presented below.

Positive emotion

According to Seligman, people should experience positive emotions in their lives. This can emerge from many areas of a person's life (work, relationships, hobbies etc.). Coaches can activate positive emotions by using humour during their conversations, encouraging playfulness and highlighting opportunities to celebrate successes.

Engagement

In order to experience wellbeing, people need to be engaged. It is important that people are engaging in meaningful tasks and activities. Human beings can experience flow (Csikszentmihalyi, 1990) when they engage in activities that are challenging and enjoyable. To increase the sense of engagement, coaches can encourage their coachees to select personally challenging goals, include absorbing creative tasks during the coaching sessions or suggest immersive activities to undertake in between meetings.

Positive relationships

Because human beings are social animals, they need to have positive relationships in their lives. These can span personal and professional domains, including lovers, friends, colleagues, family members and acquaintances. Coaches can raise the profile of personal and professional relationships by asking about their coachees' networks and trying to understand team and organisational dynamics.

Meaning

According to Seligman's PERMA theory, human beings need to have a purpose in life. It is important for people to feel that their lives are meaningful in some way. 'Research is consistent in affirming that meaning in life is part of the complex picture of human wellbeing and optimal functioning' (Steger, 2009: 680). Coaches can explicitly ask questions about their coachees' purpose in life and help them to explain how their goals are personally meaningful. According to Kate Hefferon and Ilona Boniwell, 'It is also the actual progression towards the goal and not necessarily the attainment of the goal that creates wellbeing ... Goals add structure and meaning to our daily life, helping us learn how to manage our time ... People with aspirations and dreams that are in progress or achievable and are personally meaningful, are happier than those that do not have them' (2011: 137).

Accomplishment

Human beings can only flourish if they experience a sense of accomplishment. This accomplishment can come from achieving meaningful tasks or working towards important objectives. Coaches can support their coachees by asking about recent accomplishments, reminding them of notable achievements and encouraging them to set achievable tasks to complete in between meetings.

Broaden-and-build theory

Based on decades of research and a career studying positive emotions, Barbara Fredrickson has put forward the broaden-and-build theory. Fredrickson has shown that the experience of positive emotions can have longer-term beneficial effects on human beings (2001, 2004). In fact, according to Fredrickson, there are three benefits from experiencing positive emotions. First, positive emotions allow people to think more creatively and flexibly by broadening their attention. Second, experiencing positive emotions can reduce (or 'undo') the effects of negative emotions. Third, those who experience positive emotions more regularly are likely to be more resilient during challenging times. This means that advanced practitioners should actively support coachees to experience positive emotions during the coaching conversations and in their everyday lives. For example, coaches can use humour, select inspiring locations for coaching meetings and find out more about what their coachees love to do.

Universal elements of wellbeing

From a global study covering over 150 countries, Tom Rath and Jim Harter have proposed five 'universal elements of wellbeing that differentiate a thriving life from one spent suffering' (2010: 5). Importantly, the elements describe aspects that people can do something about. According to Rath and Harter, the five elements of wellbeing are: career, social, financial, physical and community (2010). Each will be discussed below.

- *Career wellbeing* is the extent to which people enjoy what they typically do on most days of their lives. So, it is not narrowly focused on professional careers, but on the roles that people undertake on a day-to-day basis. Rath and Harter argue that 'boosting ... career wellbeing might be one of the most important priorities to consider for maintaining good health over the years' (p. 25). Career wellbeing predicts better wellbeing across the other four elements (listed below).
- *Social wellbeing* is about a person's relationships and social networks. As social beings, people get a sense of wellbeing from feeling connected. According to Rath and Harter, people who are thriving in this element 'have several close relationships that help them achieve, enjoy life, and be healthy. They are surrounded by people who encourage their development and growth' (p. 44).
- *Financial wellbeing* relates to a person's level of satisfaction with her standard of living. Rath and Harter conclude that 'the amount of money you have ... is not the best gauge of ... financial wellbeing' (p. 49). Rather, people feel better when they are satisfied with their standard of living, believe that they are financially secure, give to others and use their money to create time for what is important.
- *Physical wellbeing* is the extent to which people believe that they are healthy. Rath and Harter particularly focus on exercise, eating habits and sleeping patterns. By getting the right balance and lifestyle, it is possible for people to feel better on a daily basis and also protect against illness in later life.
- *Community wellbeing* includes a basic sense of security in one's community, but also relates to the extent that a person feels that she is 'giving back' to her community. Rath and Harter argue that 'this element can actually be *the differentiator between a good life and a great one*' (p. 93).

Focus on practice: Building positive psychology interventions into coaching conversations

In addition to adapting practices and questions based on relevant positive psychology theories, it is also possible to use positive psychology interventions (PPIs) to enhance the subjective wellbeing of coachees. These can be incorporated into the coaching conversations or agreed as tasks in between coaching sessions. The most relevant interventions are described below.

(Continued)

(Continued)

Three good things journal

This requires the coachee to reflect on her day every night for a week. Just before going to sleep, the coachee should write in a journal about three good things that happened on that day. In addition to thinking about these things, the coachee should reflect on her own part in that positive experience.

The gratitude email

This intervention will require the coachee to spend some time reflecting on personal or professional relationships. The coachee is asked to think about a person that she appreciates at home or at work. When she has identified someone, she should compose an email (or letter) that details exactly what she appreciates about the other person. The original PPI requires that the letter is read out loud in the presence of the other person. If this is too much of a challenge, it can be sent as an email!

Identifying signature strengths

When a person is aware of her strengths and uses them more broadly in her daily life, she is more likely experience higher levels of subjective wellbeing (Peterson and Seligman, 2004). Coachees can benefit from completing an online survey of their signature strengths (www.viacharacter.org). Once the coachee has completed the survey, the advanced practitioner can work with her to think of how to use her signature strengths in new and innovative ways in more areas of her life.

Understanding time perspective

The concept of time perspective relates to a psychological (and therefore subjective) sense of time. According to psychologists Philip Zimbardo and John Boyd, a person's time perspective may have an effect on every decision that she makes. Zimbardo and Boyd have shown that people have preferred time perspectives (1999). For example, people who have a preference for the past may enjoy thinking positively about their childhood (reminiscing) while others who have a preference for the future are likely to be thinking about upcoming events and goals most of the time. A person's preferred time perspectives can strongly influence her sense of wellbeing (1999). Therefore, coachees can be invited to complete the Zimbardo time perspective inventory (ZTPI) to get a better understanding of their own preferences. According to the ZTPI, there are particular time perspectives that are better for a person's wellbeing. Advanced practitioners can therefore work with coachees to discuss their coachees' time perspectives and explore whether this can be adapted.

Integrating positive psychology into advanced coaching practice

In this chapter, we have considered the challenge of supporting a coachee to achieve important goals while also prioritising her wellbeing. Advanced practitioners should work to minimise any tension between the two. Both success and wellbeing are positive outcomes, and each should enhance the other. We have argued for the benefits of integrating positive psychology theories and interventions into effective coaching practice. While some might call this 'positive psychology coaching', we consider this to be advanced coaching practice. By remembering the fundamental importance of the purpose of coaching to enhance both the performance and wellbeing of our clients, advanced practice should allow the following to happen:

- the coachee feels valued ('I feel listened to')
- the coachee experiences a sense of autonomy ('I have choices')
- the coachee believes that the coach cares about her wellbeing ('I am cared for')
- the coachee feels confident ('I have strengths')
- the coachee feels resourceful ('I can build on my previous successes')
- the coachee experiences hopefulness ('My future will be better than the present')
- the coachee feels efficacious ('I can make this happen')
- the coach has self-belief ('I think I will be able to do this').

By prioritising the wellbeing of their coachees, advanced practitioners create the conditions in which meaningful goals can be achieved successfully and sustainably.

10
BEING IMPARTIAL AND STRENGTHENING HOPEFULNESS

Visit https://study.sagepub.com/advancedcoaching to watch the videos discussed in this chapter:

VIDEO 10.1: Using strengths cards to instil hope
VIDEO 10.2: Highlighting coachee's energy to instil hope
VIDEO 10.3: Getting the coachee to focus on the positive

While impartiality and professional detachment underpin effective coaching practice, at its heart, coaching is an intervention designed to increase hopefulness. Advanced practitioners will be aware of their role in instilling hope into coaching conversations. One way of evaluating the success of coaching is to determine if coachees are more hopeful at the end of a coaching conversation than before it. Of course, there may be exceptions to this way of evaluating coaching. Due to the personalised nature of coaching, there will be times when coachees may need to reassess or temper their aspirations. However, in this chapter, we will allow our attention to be drawn to the advanced practitioner's role in supporting coachees to become more hopeful about achieving their goals.

See it in practice: Strengthening hopefulness by focusing on the positive

Video 10.1

Video 10.2

Video 10.3

In Video 10.1, Christian uses VIA (Values in Action) strengths cards to instil hope into the conversation. In Video 10.2, Jackee focuses on highlighting the coachee's energy to create hopefulness. In Video 10.3, Christian encourages the coachee to focus on the positive elements of her situation.

It is interesting to consider hopefulness in the context of introductory coach training programmes that emphasise the need for coaches to be impartial. Impartiality underpins many of the key principles of being an effective coach. First, it is argued that the coach should maintain an objective perspective. Second, the coach is advised to adopt a non-judgemental stance in relation to her coachees. Third, it is taught that coaches should not lead their coachees. These principles are widely accepted within the field and it will be helpful to explore them in further detail below.

MAINTAINING AN OBJECTIVE PERSPECTIVE

It is often argued that coaches must remain neutral and impartial during coaching conversations. The logic is that by providing an unbiased perspective, coaches allow their coachees to reflect deeply on their current contexts. Coachees are then able to check their perceptions and ideas with an objective (impartial) 'other', allowing them to refine their thinking and develop appropriate strategies for moving forward. Based on this argument, it becomes important that coaches do not 'take sides', either standing too strongly with their coachees (e.g. against perceived injustices) or supporting the organisations in which they work (e.g. taking the management viewpoint). In the early stages of their development, coaches usually find that they have to temper their desire to *over-empathise* with their coachees. In some cases, novice coaches may inadvertently be making the situation more challenging by encouraging their coachees to be inflexible and less open-minded in the face of challenges and opportunities. For all of these reasons, it has become accepted that coaches should strive to be impartial and unbiased. However, in this chapter, we will propose that advanced practitioners should not be entirely impartial.

ADOPTING A NON-JUDGEMENTAL STANCE

The idea of a coach needing to maintain a non-judgemental stance is discussed in Chapter 7 (Being ethical and staying true to personal values). In brief, this principle relates to creating the conditions in which the coachee can be open and honest. If coaches remain non-judgmental during coaching conversations, this encourages their coachees to share their thoughts more freely. If, on the other hand, a coachee feels judged by her coach, she is less likely to be completely honest. While many coaches will immediately recognise the importance of being non-judgemental as a coach, it is another matter altogether to *become* less judgemental. This is why we consider this to be more about a 'coaching way of being' than a skill. The critical outcome is that the coachee does not *feel* judged by her coach. Any indication that the coach is making a negative judgement about the behaviour, views, thoughts or background of the coachee is detrimental to the coaching relationship and is likely to disrupt any sense of safety that may have been created.

BEING NON-DIRECTIVE

Based on the humanistic roots of coaching, the importance of being non-directive is highlighted in most coach training programmes. Contemporary coaching practice adopts one aspect of Carl Rogers' (1961) principle of non-directivity. Somewhat ironically, trainee coaches are *told* that they should not 'tell' their coachees what to do because coaching is an interaction that respects autonomy. Often, this runs counter to a perceived 'default position' in professional contexts that helpful managers should solve problems faced by their staff. Further, it is still widely accepted that managers and supervisors should direct their staff, tell them what to do, and advise them on how to do their jobs. The moment participants of introductory coach training programmes realise that coaching advocates the opposite approach is often a significant one. Participants start to explore non-directivity tentatively, often doubting that such an approach can be effective. Coach training programmes aim to broaden their participants' repertoires, presenting directive to non-directive interventions as a spectrum. Given that many participants will be more familiar with interventions towards the directive end of the spectrum, the training tends to focus on non-directive ways of supporting others. In practice, this means that trainee coaches experiment with allowing coachees to develop their own solutions and ideas without interference. For example, introductory coach training programmes teach learners not to use 'leading questions' (questions that lead the coachee in a particular direction), favouring open questions where possible. It is taught that open questions encourage openness, reflection and exploration and that leading questions are an attempt to influence coachees. So, the intention of teaching 'non-directivity' to trainee coaches is to allow them to be able to listen and be present without guiding their coachees towards predetermined goals and solutions. In summary, contemporary practice in coaching promotes the notion of impartiality. Accordingly, coaches are advised to adopt a 'neutral' stance, making sure not to become too attached. Further, in order to create a conducive environment for thinking, trainee coaches are advised to remain non-judgemental and ensure that they do not tell their coachees what to do.

REASSESSING IMPARTIALITY AND THE 'NECESSARY CONDITIONS'

Some important questions arise when considering the contemporary views discussed above. On the issue of impartiality, is it actually in the best interest of the coachee? The risk of the coach appearing to be completely impartial is that she may seem distant and uncaring. Given that coaching is intended to be an encouraging, positive conversation, such impartiality may give the impression that the coach lacks empathy. Perhaps it may be more helpful for advanced practitioners to focus on 'objectivity' rather than 'impartiality'. Coaches add value when they bring a sense of objectivity to a conversation. Objectivity allows coaches to see things from multiple perspectives.

This means that advanced practitioners support their coachees by being relatively objective while also demonstrating empathy for the coachee. In fact, the most effective coaching relationships will be based on the coachee's perception that her coach is alongside her and supportive. It is more important for the coachee to feel that the coach cares about her than for the coach to be impartial. In fact, the coachee must be convinced that her coach is always working in *her* best interest. When a coach challenges the coachee, it should be clear that she is doing so because she believes that this is in the best interest of the coachee – not because the coach is simply being coldly impartial.

Another question to consider is the extent to which the 'necessary conditions' for counselling apply to coaching. Originally titled 'The necessary and sufficient conditions of therapeutic personality change' (1957), Rogers was specifically discussing their use in counselling, or therapeutic conversations. There is no doubt that coaching and counselling have a common history. They share many similarities: both are helping conversations; both involve two people talking about what one of them will do to overcome challenges or move towards a desired outcome; in both cases, the practitioner should be skilled at supporting the client. These similarities make it logical to assume that the 'necessary conditions' for counselling might also be the basis for coaching conversations.

However, Rogers' concept of non-directivity extends beyond 'not telling the client what to do' and applies to the conversational process itself. In other words, a non-directive practitioner would not even 'manage' the conversational process. This is where contemporary coaching practice diverges from Rogers' view. Whereas Rogers argued that creating the right conditions (which included non-directivity) was necessary *and sufficient*, most coach training programmes imply that creating these conditions is desirable *but not sufficient*. In other words, training programmes teach that coaches should work towards creating the right climate for their coachees, but then suggest that more is needed. In contemporary practice, there is a tendency towards more active involvement of the coach once a conducive environment has been created. Most coaches take a proactive role in encouraging their coachees to develop strategies and tactics to move closer to their desired goals. In fact, much of the training in introductory coaching programmes revolves around training in the use and management of conversational processes such as GROW (Whitmore, 1992). Trainee coaches are taught that it is both their role and their responsibility to manage the coaching conversation within an agreed amount of time. Coachees are taken through the conversational process, and encouraged, coaxed and nudged by their coaches to set targets and commit to actions.

Out of this debate arises a particular challenge for the advanced practitioner: respecting the autonomy and independence of the coachee whilst acknowledging that leading becomes inevitable when managing a coaching conversation (see Chapter 5: Being tenacious and encouraging autonomy). By taking the coaching conversation in one direction or another, the advanced practitioner is leading the coachee by drawing her attention to a certain aspect of the topic. Every question posed by the coach is 'leading' inasmuch as it directs the coachee to think in a particular way. But there may be even more subtle ways of leading a coachee. If coaches seem to favour one line of thinking by being enthusiastic about it, this can also be a form of leading. For example, saying 'I like your thinking, tell me more about that' suggests approval and is likely to encourage the coachee to pursue that line of thinking further. Equally, simply being more enthusiastic about some options may cause the coachee to select them over those options about which the coach was less enthusiastic.

Even more problematically, it soon becomes apparent to coaches that the intention of being non-judgmental is practically impossible to achieve. We have proposed earlier that coaches often manage the conversational process. This requires the use of judgement by the coach: when to move from one stage to another; how to introduce a technique; how to raise the coachee's awareness; whether it is culturally appropriate to provide feedback and so on. These are just a few examples. Viewed from this perspective, making such judgements is core to the role of an effective coach, and these judgements are being made throughout any coaching conversation. Not only that, coaches make judgements *about* the coachee herself: how open she may be to challenge; whether she is engaged in the topic of conversation; or how committed she is to undertake the actions identified during the session. So, while the coach cannot be said to be non-judgemental, it is important that the coachee *feels* that she is not being judged about who she is, her perspective, her decisions, how she lives her life or what she wants to work towards.

In conclusion, advanced practitioners tend to focus on objectivity rather than impartiality so that they are able to demonstrate care and empathy for their coachees whilst also maintaining a level of professional detachment that allows them to consider multiple perspectives and viewpoints. Advanced practitioners may use Rogers' necessary and sufficient conditions as a basis for creating positive relationships with their coachees. However, they are also aware of the fact that they should be more active conversational partners. Advanced practitioners must manage the delicate balance between respecting the autonomy and the independence of their coachees whilst being an active conversational partner. On the one hand, as we have discussed above, it is important for the coach to be as non-judgemental as possible and try not to lead the coachee's thinking too much whilst leading the conversational process. On the other, advanced practitioners recognise that the purpose of coaching is to increase hopefulness. Below, we will consider theories about optimism and hope.

TWO THEORIES OF OPTIMISM

The first theory to consider is 'learned optimism' (Seligman, 1991). After researching the phenomenon of animals that give up trying because they learn that they have no control (learned helplessness), Seligman turned his attention to learned optimism. From the 'learned optimism perspective, therefore, the optimistic goal-directed cognitions are aimed at distancing the person from negative outcomes of high importance' (Lopez, Pedrotti & Snyder, 2015: 193). In other words, Seligman studied optimism by finding out how people explained negative events. According to his theory, optimists and pessimists have different ways of explaining negative events. Optimists tend to respond to them with external attribution, variable attribution and specific attribution. This means that an optimist thinks in a way that attributes negative events to external factors (external attribution), considers such events as less likely in the future (variable attribution) and limits negative experiences to particular areas of their life (specific attribution). On the other hand, a pessimist thinks in a way that attributes negative events to personal weaknesses or limitations (internal attribution), believes that such events are likely to recur (stable attribution) and expects these events to negatively impact all aspects of her life (global attribution) (see the 'Story from our practice' below for examples). To put it simply, optimists and pessimists see the same events with different lenses.

Stories from our practice: Responding to negative experiences

As an example, we will take the case of a coachee not being successful at securing a more senior role within her own organisation. Due to the retirement of a senior manager, staff within the organisation were invited to apply for the role. As part of a restructuring process, the post was ringfenced to internal candidates only. For the purposes of this scenario, let us imagine that our coachee was interviewed but not selected for the role. She was told that she was unsuccessful, and a colleague of hers was offered the role.

An optimistic thought process would have these components:

- External attribution: 'Internal politics meant that I was not chosen.'
- Variable attribution: 'I have been very successful in past interviews, so this is a one-off situation. If another internal opportunity arises, I'll be likely to get it.'
- Specific attribution: 'While this interview didn't go the way I wanted, I'm doing really well in the job, and I have a great work–life balance.'

A pessimistic thought process would have these components:

- Internal attribution: 'I knew it. I'm just not good enough for such senior roles.'
- Stable attribution: 'I'm never going to be a leader. It's always going to be a stretch for me to apply for a senior management job.'
- Global attribution: 'I'm not cut out for this kind of role. I've made some bad decisions in my life, and everything seems to be going wrong for me.'

Michael Scheier and Charles Carver offer an alternative view called 'dispositional optimism' (1992). Rather than seeing optimism as a way of explaining negative events, they suggest that it is more about the level of expectation a person has in relation to reaching a goal. The key factor driving optimism is the expectation level. In fact, Scheier and Carver propose that the expectation can relate to the ability to move towards a desirable goal but could also apply to expectation about moving away from unwanted situations.

From an advanced practitioner's perspective, both theories can add value to coaching conversations. One implication is that it is worth working with the coachee on their thinking processes. By helping coachees to become aware of their preferred way of thinking about negative events, advanced practitioners can support them to think more positively about themselves, thereby increasing optimism and motivation to continue working towards important goals. Another implication is that advanced practitioners should work specifically on coachees' level of expectation about their ability to reach meaningful objectives. Research supports the use of these approaches with a number of studies suggesting that optimism can lead to improved educational and work performance, and better ability to cope with difficult situations (Carver, Scheier, Miller & Fulford, 2009).

COGNITIVE THEORY OF HOPE

According to leading academics in the field of positive psychology, hope is 'goal-directed thinking in which the person utilizes pathways thinking (the perceived capacity to find routes to desired goals) and agency thinking (the requisite motivations to use those routes)' (Lopez, Pedrotti & Snyder, 2015: 204). Charles Snyder, the founder of hope theory, was initially interested in the ways in which people make excuses and studied how people explained away negative experiences such as mistakes and failures. It was through this work that he started becoming curious about why some people made excuses while others did not. Hope theory is underpinned by the assumption that human behaviour is generally goal directed (Rand & Cheavens, 2009: 324).

Snyder proposed that hope could be generated by making a connection between the perceived present state and an imagined positive future (Lopez, Pedrotti & Snyder, 2015). The two components of his theory are 'pathways thinking' and 'agency thinking'. Pathways thinking refers to the ability of people to generate multiple ways to overcome challenges or barriers. Agency thinking is more about a person's belief that she will be able to generate alternative pathways when required. Being able to imagine multiple pathways to the imagined (positive) future has benefits emotionally (it feels like there are numerous ways of achieving a desired outcome) and practically (if one pathway is not successful, alternative routes can be attempted).

Snyder's theory applies to conscious goals that are perceived as important by those pursuing them (Lopez, Pedrotti & Snyder, 2015: 204). Goals, according to Snyder, should be classified as being either 'approach' or 'avoidance'. In other words, a person can either be working towards something (e.g. a better work–life balance) or trying to avoid something (e.g. an embarrassing experience). If a coachee says that she 'doesn't want to look silly in front of my colleagues', this would be considered an avoidance goal. By its nature, the objective is to avoid a negative outcome. Although hope can be generated for both approach and avoidance goals, advanced practitioners will support their coachees to work on approach goals as these tend to enhance wellbeing. When an avoidance goal is presented, it can be helpful to work with the coachee to reframe it into an approach goal. See the 'Focus on practice' box below for some strategies for enhancing pathways and agency thinking.

Focus on practice: Using hope theory in coaching

Jeana Magyar-Moe and Shane Lopez (2015: 496–7) have made some recommendations for enhancing pathways and agency thinking.

For pathways thinking

- Break a long-range goal into steps or subgoals.
- Practise making different routes to your goals and select the best one.
- Mentally rehearse scripts for what you would do should you encounter a blockage.

For agency thinking

- Recall your previous successful goal pursuits, particularly when you are in a jam.
- Find a substitute goal when the original goal is blocked solidly.
- Enjoy the process of getting to your goals and do not focus only on the final attainment.

When people choose to be coached, it is a fair assumption that they may be experiencing some doubt or uncertainty about their ability to achieve a particular goal, objective, intention or aspiration. Or, to look at this differently, if a person believed that her desired outcome could be achieved easily and quickly, she would be less likely to seek out the services of a coach. So, on the one hand, people are likely to come to coaching with some uncertainty or doubt about their ability to achieve their goals; on the other, it can be assumed that people who choose to be coached hope that it is possible for them to achieve their goals. This intriguing interplay between doubt and hope characterises many coaching conversations.

Focus on practice: Using hope theory in coaching

Strategies for increasing hopefulness

Highlighting resources

The coach can support the coachee by helping her to identify existing resources that can be harnessed. For example, 'What is already in place that will help you to achieve your goal?' or 'Who might be able to support you with this project?' are both questions that can increase hopefulness by raising awareness of resources that will make it easier for the coachee to achieve her goal.

Identifying options

The 'options' phase of a coaching conversation is an ideal opportunity to increase hopefulness. Often coachees can only see one or two ways of moving forward. These options tend to be suboptimal and may even have been considered before. Coaches should persist until the coachee generates some new ideas. Having between four to six options is most likely to make the coachee feel optimistic. This means that a coachee would be able to select between a number of potential ways forward. Having numerous viable options can also mean that a coachee would have alternative paths available to her should her first option not be successful.

Agreeing specific action plans

The final stage of a coaching conversation should build momentum and energy. Supporting coachees to design and commit to specific action plans is an important part of increasing hopefulness. Coaches will facilitate their coachees in developing these action plans to ensure

(Continued)

(Continued)

that they seem to be enthusiastic about the way forward. Advanced practitioners will work towards setting specific, achievable actions that can be implemented in between coaching sessions. Achieving these steps will add to the growing sense of self-efficacy and hopefulness of coachees.

Noticing and appreciating strengths

Coaches can be very encouraging and supportive by listening specifically for a coachee's strengths and playing these back. For example, 'It sounds like you have a strength in being able to forgive others. Is this something you've noticed before?' By helping coachees to appreciate their own strengths, the advanced practitioner is able to build confidence and increase hopefulness about using the strengths to overcome obstacles and challenges.

Recognising skills

As with strengths, it is also helpful for coaches to notice particular skills that the coachee has developed. For example, 'From what you've said, it seems that you're very skilled at delivering complex projects. Are there ways of using these skills in this situation?' Sometimes coachees fail to recognise their own skills and can therefore feel disempowered. By making connections between existing skills and the challenges that coachees are facing, coaches can provide reasons to be hopeful.

Recalling previous successes

A simple and powerful technique for increasing the hopefulness of coachees is to ask them to remember previous successes. For example, 'Can you recall a time when you were able to handle this kind of challenge successfully?' Past successes can provide ideas for how to tackle the current challenge – and crucially provide evidence that the coachee has the ability to overcome seemingly difficult situations. The additional insights and the track record of success will boost the hopefulness of the coachee.

Being enthusiastic and encouraging

The ideal environment for coaching conversations is supportive and encouraging. To create this positive learning environment, coaches should be enthusiastic and encouraging (e.g. 'I'm looking forward to hearing about what you've been thinking' or 'I'm getting a sense that you are very committed to making the changes you've discussed with me'). The enthusiasm should focus primarily on the coaching conversation and progress that is being made, rather than on specific options that the coachee may be considering. It is the responsibility of the coach to be consistently and relentlessly encouraging. Whether the coachee is making progress, feeling stuck or experiencing setbacks, the advanced practitioner should remain encouraging, focusing on the importance of the coaching conversation and recognising the efforts of the coachee. This enthusiastic and encouraging approach will provide another reason for the coachee to be hopeful.

Normalising the situation

Sometimes, a coachee may feel that she is alone in experiencing doubts or lack of confidence about her abilities. In this case, it is helpful for the coach to normalise the situation (e.g., 'You're concerned that your promotion will lead to strained relationships with your current team. This is relatively common in organisations – and that shift from peer to supervisor often requires sensitive management'). In one case we observed, a coach mentioned that his coachee's impostor syndrome is experienced by many senior leaders. The purpose of such comments is to reassure the coachee that she is not alone in experiencing a particular challenge, therefore providing reasons to be hopeful that the challenge can be overcome.

Imagining best possible self

Another strategy for increasing hopefulness involves the use of a validated positive psychology intervention called 'best possible self'. The purpose of this activity is to encourage the coachee to imagine her ideal future self, assuming that she has been able to achieve everything that she hopes for. The coach invites the coachee to write out or draw an image of her best possible self. During this activity, the coach would ask questions to elicit more detail and allow the coachee to become immersed in this positive image of the future. Once the best possible self has been described, the coachee will have an engaging and inspiring glimpse of what might be achievable. This becomes a powerful motivator and something to hope for.

Many experienced coaches will already be using many of the strategies described above. Some of the strategies are taught in introductory coaching programmes, and trainee coaches have opportunities to practise using them. They are presented above not as examples of advanced practice but to showcase some of the ways that experienced coaches can intentionally deploy strategies to boost the hopefulness of their coachees. Advanced practice relates to the considered and careful balancing between being objective whilst simultaneously building the hopefulness of coachees. The concept of impartiality is not helpful because, as we have argued, the coachee should feel that the coach is 'on her side'. That is why it is more helpful to talk about the coach being objective, rather than impartial. The advanced practitioner should be objective whilst also clearly wanting the coachee to be successful. In suggesting that advanced practitioners should encourage coachees, we are not advocating that coaches should be unreasonably optimistic, nor are we suggesting that they should foster naivety in their clients. Advanced practitioners would not praise or encourage their coachees without underpinning evidence. In fact, the role of the advanced practitioner is to uncover reasons (or evidence) for the coachee to be hopeful. This includes identifying personal strengths and skills of the coachee, previous positive experiences and people that can be relied upon. By helping the coachee to have an inspiring and motivating vision of the future and supporting her to put in place achievable steps towards it, the advanced practitioner allows her to have genuine reasons to hope that it is possible.

BEING OBJECTIVE AND INSTILLING HOPE IN PRACTICE

What if the coachee is already hopeful?

As mentioned earlier, if a person has requested coaching, it is likely that she is at least somewhat hopeful about making progress towards her goal. When a coachee is already hopeful, it is helpful for coaches to notice and reflect this back to the coachee: for example, 'You seem quite confident that you'll be able to achieve this' or 'I get a sense that you're feeling quite hopeful'. This affirmation will raise the coachee's awareness of her own self-belief.

What if the coachee is 'too hopeful'?

In some situations, it may be that the coachee seems overly dependent on hoping for 'things to get better' without any reasons to support this hope. For example, 'I'm just hoping that the economy will pick up, and our leadership team will change their direction.' If appropriate the coach may explore this further by asking about the source of the hopefulness, for example, 'What are the factors that are making you feel hopeful about achieving your goal?' Raising awareness about the basis of a coachee's hopefulness will allow for discussions about the extent to which the coachee has any influence or control over any of the factors. The aim of the coach would be to build the coachee's confidence that she has influence over some of the factors that are making her hopeful.

What if hope is absent?

As argued above, those who have no hope about their chances of progressing towards a goal are less likely to seek out coaching. So, in theory, this should be a relatively rare situation. However, when people have been advised or coerced to attend coaching sessions, this will be more common. In such scenarios, the coachees may not be ready to make the changes required or commit to any meaningful actions. As a consequence, they will not be hopeful about a positive outcome. When this is the case, advanced practitioners should focus on strengthening the relationship and, when appropriate, discussing the lack of hope with the coachee. This may raise awareness about the issue of readiness for coaching. If the coachee is not hopeful about making progress towards the initially identified goal, it may be worthwhile to work towards an alternative, related goal that seems more achievable. This strategy can be helpful in building trust between the coach and the coachee, and could provide evidence of the value of coaching conversations. Both of these factors could then be the basis for increasing the readiness of the coachee for further conversations.

What about the hopefulness of the coach?

The hopefulness of the coach is a critical success factor in coaching. As we will discuss later, this should be part of the 'coaching way of being'. In one way or another, it is necessary for the coach to be genuinely hopeful about the ability of her coachees to make progress towards their goals.

Focus on practice: Possible sources of the hopefulness of coaches

- Previous and continuing experience of coaching.
- Ongoing reflexivity aimed at improving coaching practice.
- Ability to create safe learning environments.
- Skill in managing complex conversations.
- Growing awareness and confidence in one's coaching way of being.

11
BEING

Both of us are lifelong learners, and we are fascinated with coaching. This rewarding writing project has accelerated our learning and has amplified our curiosity about advanced practice. At the start of this book we had proposed that 'advanced coaching practice' might have something to do with a coach's 'way of being' – how she is in the room with her coachee, the relationship she builds and sustains with her coachee, and what she brings of herself to that relationship. We started our exploration by suggesting that coaching might be a craft (i.e. an activity that involves skill in producing outputs of some kind). In the case of coaching, the outcomes are actions, changed behaviour or improved performance. Now, at this stage of our project, we are increasingly drawn to the idea that advanced practice might be an art (i.e. an activity which involves the application of human creative skill and imagination, and through practice elevates those skills to very high levels of proficiency). Advanced practice embodies a sense of beauty and wonder that enables people to see themselves, their relationships with others and the worlds they inhabit more clearly – the elements within and around them that they shape, and are shaped by, akin to the interplay of the light with the subjects of photographs.

In Chapter 1 (The complexity of advanced coaching practice) we outlined a framework that set out to capture the key elements of a coach's growth and development from trainee to experienced practitioner. Reflecting on this framework we believe it remains a helpful way to illustrate the key phases of coach development, with the caveat that individual coaches' growth will take their own personal routes. However, it seems ironic that initial coach development, while often participatory and interactive, still relies to a significant degree on taught components, particularly in relation to the various models for approaching coaching conversations and the core skills. This seems in sharp contrast to the essence of coaching, which rightly emphasises the autonomy and expertise of the coachee. In our own coach development work we will endeavour to find even more ways to ensure that the experience of learning about coaching more closely resembles the art of coaching itself.

Coaches are sometimes referred to as 'catalysts' in that they create the conditions for something productive to happen. This is clearly true as far as it goes. However, the scientific definition of a catalyst is a substance that enables a chemical reaction to take place without succumbing to any change itself. Here is where the catalyst metaphor ceases to be helpful. As we know from our own experience and from working with other coaches, each coaching encounter also has an impact on the coach, perhaps in terms of learning about our art, enhancing our understanding of people, or experiencing a human, emotional response. Coaching is clearly focused on enabling another person to achieve her desired outcomes. It is, then, all about the coachee – and for coaching conversations to be successful, we believe, it is crucially also all about the coach in the sense of what she brings of herself, her expertise and her experiences to the relationship.

OUR NOTION OF ADVANCED COACHING PRACTICE

In this book, we've proposed that advanced practitioners should focus on the process whilst prioritising the coaching relationship at the same time. We've explored the need for coaches to be challenging whilst also arguing that coaches must be willing to let things go. We believe that coaches must be able to acknowledge the wider system but that it is important that they are fully present in the coaching conversation. Coaches, we argue, have to be persistent in the pursuit of goals whilst simultaneously respecting the autonomy of their coachees. To bring creativity into coaching conversations, advanced practitioners must build and maintain trust with their coachees. Being ethical as a coach is non-negotiable, but she must also stay true to her own deeply held values. Advanced practitioners have to find ways to be authentic whilst adapting to meet the needs of their coachees. The successful performance of coachees is one of the driving forces of coaching, but we argue that advanced practitioners must also prioritise the wellbeing of those that they work with. And whilst advanced practitioners should maintain professional detachment and remain impartial, they are also responsible for instilling hope into their coaching conversations.

What we have learned

So, what have we learned as we grappled with the notion of advanced practice? Most importantly, the process has reaffirmed our commitment to strong, mutually respectful and productive relationships as the foundation of coaching practice. These powerful, co-created relationships are at the heart of transformational coaching conversations. This is why advanced practice can be understood as an art that relies on a sophisticated use of core coaching skills and the flexible, coachee-centred application of a conversational framework delivered by an authentic person. Although coaching should be a professional, managed conversation, advanced practitioners move beyond linear, transactional engagement. Coachees should experience what feels like a dialogue. However, it should not sound like one. What we mean by this is that it won't sound like a dialogue because the coachee does most of the talking. She has come to the realisation, through experience with the coach, that the session is about her. It is her time. The conversation feels like a dialogue because both parties know that they have a voice and both feel fully engaged in the conversation. Both coach and coachee are of equal value, and the conversation progresses in a way that is free, exploratory and developmental because both parties feel trusted and respected. It should feel like a conversation between two autonomous, independent and competent adults, because that's exactly what it is.

Of course, coaching is a conversation about growth and development, but advanced practice is more than that. Advanced practitioners lead conversations that incorporate meaning and purpose. Coachees talk about what is important. It leads them to consider their potential, to imagine the best version of themselves. Such conversations provide an opportunity for people to align themselves with their values and to strive towards meaningful goals and intentions. Coaching is perfectly suited to human beings who are meaning-making creatures. By reminding coachees of what is possible, coaching conversations can stimulate hope that they can have greater agency in their lives.

In this book, we have intentionally kept the focus on positive outcomes for coachees. But what about coaches? When we argued that the advanced practitioner should prioritise the wellbeing of their coachees, we did not talk about the wellbeing of the coach. When we mentioned above that advanced practice might stimulate hope that it is possible to have greater agency, we were talking about the coachee. To what extent is it important that advanced practitioners have meaningful and positive intentions too? What expectation is there that advanced practitioners should be striving to raise their own self-awareness and continue to work towards personal development?

KEY QUALITIES OF THE ADVANCED PRACTITIONER

There is growing discussion in the field about a coaching 'way of being'. With the title of this final chapter we clearly see ourselves in this territory too and are convinced that a coach's way of being, alongside the doing, thinking and feeling involved in coaching, is at the heart of advanced coaching practice. In bringing together our thoughts about advanced practice there is a danger that we appear to be replicating the very kind of taxonomy or competency framework that we have described as useful but ultimately limited. Our intention here is to identify some qualities and characteristics of advanced practitioners that have emerged to date from our learning. This is a work in progress for us, which is inevitably constrained by the physical and time-bound nature of a book format. With those important caveats, we believe that it may be helpful for readers of this book to consider our conclusions about the concept of advanced practice.

In the presence of the advanced practitioner, coachees may:

- increase their enthusiasm for the journey
- gain clarity about their destination(s)
- become more curious about what can be learned along the way
- start to enjoy the journey more
- become more thoughtful about when to rest
- have an increased understanding of what has been learned
- access personal resources and resilience
- become courageous about decisions that need to be made.

Let's start with a clear baseline, which is rightly included in all thinking about good practice in coaching. We should be very clear: all coaches, including advanced practitioners, should be qualified and adept at the effective use of the core coaching skills. The advanced practitioner believes in the centrality of the coaching relationship and in continuous contracting to ensure that conversations stay on track. She has a high degree of self-awareness. She is able to manage her emotions well. She is actively committed to reflective practice, engaged in regular supervision in some form and is a lifelong learner. Beyond this baseline the advanced practitioner, with greater and greater experience, will see her proficiency in all these areas become increasingly sophisticated and attuned to the diverse needs of her coachees. She is a consummate builder and sustainer of productive coaching relationships, recognising that this is *the* vital ingredient for successful coaching. Again, with expanding experience she is becoming increasingly sophisticated and sensitive in creating the relationships that work for a diverse range of coachees. These relationships are characterised by humility, honesty, trust and frankness in the service of her coachees.

The advanced practitioner is fully present in the room with her coachee and is curious about what motivates her coachee as well as the proactive, and reactive, interactions the coachee has with the worlds around her. The advanced practitioner is less interested in the facts of a situation presented by a coachee being much more focused on patterns in, for example, language, metaphors, thinking, emotional factors, beliefs and behaviour and what they suggest about about the coachee's engagement with the world. She is clear about her own values and is able to draw on these for the benefit of her coachees. She is open-minded and able to work with people who hold different values to her own, acknowledging how her own 'red buttons' might be triggered and working sensitively in the moment to manage their impacts. The advanced practitioner moves beyond a focus on the presenting issue, subtly and appropriately balancing behaviour with consideration of the values, beliefs, intentions and assumptions that underpin coachees' actions.

The advanced practitioner has a clear picture of her own philosophy of life, which she endeavours not to impose on others. She knows her limitations and how these affect what she promises in coaching contracts. She is clear about how these limitations impact particular coaching relationships and works, through supervision and continuous reflection and learning to mitigate them.

The advanced practitioner has strong self-belief and confidence in her ability to create safe, transformational thinking spaces and adopts a relentless collaborative and appreciative stance to her coaching. She uses a variety of processes with subtlety and sensitivity, adjusting her approach to bring the appropriate balance of support and challenge to each conversation. She uses process to facilitate deeper engagement with coachees, rather than as a substitute for being accurately attentive about what might work best in each individual circumstance.

The advanced practitioner is appropriately authentic, drawing on her own personal resources as a potential source of growth for her coachees. She draws on her own professional and personal experience judiciously to strengthen the relationship and to offer possible ideas for how coachees might progress with their goals. The advanced practitioner has a good understanding of her own creative interests, be they in the field of the arts, sciences or hobbies, and how they might be used to unlock the potential of her coachees. She uses a range of eclectic coaching methods and her confidence in bringing them to the attention of her coachees is a major source of the positive energy required to enable those methods to succeed, even with participants who are taking tentative first steps towards change. There will be occasions where the advanced practitioner experiences the state of flow in her work – where she is so engaged with her coachee in the moment that the questions, lines of inquiry and challenges seem to appear from nowhere.

The advanced practitioner draws on learning and methods from other disparate fields to enable coachees to discover new ways of seeing. She presents coaching methods and other relevant frameworks simply, without diminishing the complexity of the topics brought to conversations by coachees and applies these in a holistic way in her work.

The advanced practitioner, based on the trusting relationships she builds, is able to robustly challenge coachees when this is appropriate. She presents challenges in respectful and elegant ways that enable coachees to face the implications constructively. She knows that a well-crafted, clear and quietly tenacious challenge can be more difficult for coachees to side-step than outright confrontation.

She brings an appropriate energy to coaching conversations, for example, bringing calmness and stillness when coachees are flustered and hyperactive, through matching their moods when that feels productive, to injecting pace into conversations where coachees are downbeat and lacking the necessary verve to make the desired move forward. The advanced practitioner is also comfortable with silence, uncertainty, disharmony and high emotions, whether they be positive or negative.

The advanced practitioner is inclusive in her approach to coaching, both in relation to working with coachees from a diverse range of backgrounds and worldviews and to the colleagues those coachees discuss during coaching conversations. She is able to work effectively with people from a wide range of backgrounds and with a range of life experiences. Working with sensitivity she recognises that, while those backgrounds and experiences have impacts, everyone is an individual with their own particular perspective on how those impacts shape their lives. The advanced practitioner sees her coachees, for example, as sources of cultural knowledge in the room, meaning she feels no need to make assumptions about experiences that are very different from her own. She acknowledges and works effectively with the power dynamics inherent in systems, including the system that is the relationship between coach and coachee, and the sponsor. In specific situations she is alert to the sources of authority that arise from differences in experiences, backgrounds and characteristics. She has an interest in, and some understanding of, human interactions at individual and organisational levels, without needing to be a trained psychologist or sociologist.

In short, the advanced practitioner has given thought to, and has established her own personal way of being as a coach developed through self-reflection, and she keeps her approach under regular review.

FINAL THOUGHTS: EXAMINING THE METAPHOR OF THE COACHING JOURNEY

Despite its well-worn use in the coaching literature, we believe that this metaphor remains helpful for understanding the complexities and richness of coaching. Every conversation should feel like a conversation between two human beings that are on their separate journeys but are walking together for a while. Advanced practice is characterised by mutual humanity, mutual respect and a recognition that each is interested in betterment, improvement, development or fulfilment. While the coach is a walking companion the coaching conversation should focus entirely on the journey of the coachee. Advanced practitioners will be on their own journeys towards meaningful goals, and they will have had the opportunity of walking alongside many coachees on many different journeys. Advanced practitioners use this to bring empathy, compassion, confidence and open-mindedness to every conversation. Empathy and compassion are strengthened because the advanced practitioner has recent and relevant experience of being on such journeys of discovery; confidence in the process and open-mindedness emerge from having walked alongside many different people on a broad range of individual journeys. Advanced practitioners are therefore able to better empathise with people who are clarifying their own worldviews, determining their aspirations, reflecting on their personal impact in the world, because they are doing the same. How a worldview develops, how an aspiration is shaped, these things may or may not be relevant depending on the particular circumstances – that the advanced practitioner is also on a journey is essential. It is important that the coach is walking her own path. And in many cases, it will be helpful for the coach to acknowledge that reality to herself and to her coachee, and that she has her own companions who join her along the way.

The advanced practitioner makes it clear that she will be joining for a short portion of the journey. She is a companion, someone who will walk alongside and listen, ask questions and hold up a mirror. Someone to share reflections with. The coach is not *just a companion* who tags along for the journey. She is not a *Sherpa* who guides the coachee. She has not walked along this particular path before. She does not carry the coachee's baggage along the route, or run ahead to check there are no dangers or make sure that there will be a hot cup of tea awaiting at the next rest stop. She is not a *cheerleader*, cheering and whooping to motivate the coachee. She is not a *sports coach* barking orders from the touch line. She is a *thinking partner* who walks alongside the coachee. Every coachee has her own path. However, the coach knows what it is like to persevere on the path when tired. She knows that it is important, at certain points, to slow down. She has experienced the challenge of selecting the right path when there is a fork in the road. She knows how awe-inspiring it is to come across a spectacular view. She knows when it's better to walk in silence or when it is important to sit down to catch one's breath.

Putting it into practice: Some final questions to consider

Based on your reflections from reading this book and your experiences as a coach:

- What do you know for sure about coaching?
- What are you becoming more curious about?
- What do you still need to consider and explore?
- What is unique about your own way of being as a coach?
- What is important for you?

EPILOGUE

> Visit https://study.sagepub.com/advancedcoaching to listen to Christian and David's discussion about the process of co-writing this book.

Figure 12.1

As we reflect on the process of writing this book, we appreciate the opportunity that it has given us to explore our own practice and question some of our own assumptions. We are both followers of the BBC/British Library programme *The Listening Project,* which captures conversations between two people about a significant aspect of their lives and their relationship. Our own learning is at the heart of our book and we feel that the process has strengthened our friendship too. As a way of sharing our reflections about the writing process, we thought it might be interesting to adopt *The Listening Project* format to do this.

Our informal conversation focuses on the development of our ideas about the shape and structure of the book, and on the collaborative process we established to produce the manuscript. It is important to note that we are not intending to continue our thinking about advanced practice. What we currently think about the notion of advanced practice ended in Chapter 11 (Being). We have produced an audio recording as a way for us to capture our reflections about the writing process, and we include it in the supporting materials for readers who are interested in this perspective. It is an 'optional extra' that stands alone from the content of our book. If you are interested in hearing this, please go to the link above. We have not transcribed the recording to include the text because we believe the 'live' nature of the conversation is a vital ingredient in our reflections.

Audio

As lifelong learners, writing this book and reflecting on the process in the recorded conversation has been an invaluable part of our own growth as coaches, supervisors and coach developers. Over the years we have been aspiring to incorporate the qualities and skills we explore in the book into our practice. Writing this book has redoubled our commitment and efforts to make continuing progress with that aspiration.

REFERENCES

Antonioni, D. (1998). Relationship between the Big Five personality factors and conflict management styles. *International Journal of Conflict Management*, 9(4), 336–355.

Aquilina, E. (2016). *Embodying Authenticity: A Somatic Path to Transforming Self, Team and Organisation*. London: Live It Publishing.

Association for Coaching (2017). AC Coaching Competency Framework. Available at https://c.ymcdn.com/sites/associationforcoaching.site-ym.com/resource/resmgr/Accreditation/Accred_General/Coaching_Competency_Framewor.pdf (accessed 23 October 2017).

Association for Professional Executive Coaching and Supervision (2016). APECS Ethical Guidelines. Available at www.apecs.org/ethical-guidelines (accessed 13 December 2018).

Bachkirova, T., Cox, E., & Clutterbuck, D. (2014). Introduction. In E. Cox, T. Bachkirova and D. Clutterbuck (eds), *The Complete Handbook of Coaching*, 2nd edn. London: Sage. pp. 1–18.

Bachkirova, T., Jackson, P., & Clutterbuck, D. (2011). *Coaching and Mentoring Supervision: Theory and Practice*. Maidenhead: Open University Press.

Badonsky, J. (2010). *The Nine Modern Day Muses (and a Bodyguard): Ten Guides to Creative Inspiration*, 3rd edn. San Diego, CA: Renegade Muses.

Berne, E. (1969). *A Layman's Guide to Psychiatry and Psychoanalysis*. London: Penguin Books.

Binney, G., Wilke, G., & Williams, C. (2009). *Living Leadership: A Practical Guide for Ordinary Heroes*. Harlow, ND: FT Prentice Hall.

Blakey, I. (2016). *The Trusted Executive: Nine Leadership Habits that Inspire Results, Relationships and Reputation*. London: Kogan Page.

Blakey, J., & Day, I. (2012). *Challenging Coaching: Going Beyond Traditional Coaching to Face the FACTS*. London: Nicholas Brealey.

Block, P. (2001). *The Flawless Consulting Fieldbook and Companion: A Guide to Understanding Your Expertise*. San Francisco, CA: Pfeiffer.

Blyth, D., Olson, B., & Walker, K. (2017). *Ways of Being: A Model for Social and Emotional Learning*. Youth Development Issue Brief, University of Minnesota.

Boniwell, I. (2012). *Positive Psychology in a Nutshell: The Science of Happiness*, 3rd edn. Maidenhead: Open University Press.

Bossons, P., Kourdi, J., & Sartain, D. (2012). *Coaching Essentials: Practical, Proven Techniques for World-class Executive Coaching*, 2nd edn. London: Bloomsbury.

Brennan, D., & Wildflower, L. (2010). Ethics in coaching. In E. Cox, T. Bachkirova, & D. Clutterbuck (eds). *A Complete Handbook of Coaching*. London: Sage. pp. 369–380.

Bridges, W. (2009). *Managing Transitions: Making the Most of Change*. London: Nicholas Brealey.

Brockbank, A., & McGill, I. (2012) *Facilitating Reflective Learning: Coaching, Mentoring and Supervision*, 2nd edn. London: Kogan Page.

Brown, M. (2016). Film director calls for image-based cinema, *The Guardian* (14 April 2014).

Brown, P., & Busby-Earle, D. (2014). Neurobehavioural modelling: Applying neuroscience research to the development of coaching practice. In J. Passmore (ed). *Mastery in Coaching: A Complete Psychological Toolkit for Advanced Coaching*. London: Kogan Page. pp. 127–150.

Caruso, D.R., & Salovey, P. (2004). *The Emotionally Intelligent Manager: How to Develop and Use the Four Key Emotional Skills of Leadership*. San Francisco, CA: Jossey-Bass.

Carver, C. Scheier, M., Miller, C., & Fulford, D. (2009). Optimism. In S. Lopez & C. Snyder (eds), *The Oxford Handbook of Positive Psychology*, 2nd edn. Oxford: Oxford University Press. pp. 303–311.

Cavicchia, S., & Gilbert, M. (2019). *The Theory and Practice of Relational Coaching: Complexity, Paradox and Integration*. Abingdon: Routledge.

Clutterbuck, D. (2007). *Coaching the Team at Work*. London: Nicholas Brearley.

Clutterbuck, D. (2017). *FKT Isn't Mentoring*. LinkedIn post, 24 November 2017.

Colzato, L. S., Ozturk, A., & Hommel, B. (2012). Meditate to create: The impact of focused attention and open-monitoring training on convergent and divergent thinking. *Frontiers in Psychology 3*: 116.

Cooperrider, D. L., & Whitney, D. (2008). *A Positive Revolution in Change: Appreciative Inquiry*. San Francisco, CA: Berrett-Kohler.

Cornish, T. (2009). Coaching black British coachees. In J. Passmore (ed.), *Diversity in Coaching: Working with Gender, Culture, Race and Age*. London: Kogan Page. pp. 165–180.

Csikszentmihalyi, M. (1990). *Flow: The Psychology of Optimal Experience*. New York: Harper and Row.

Csikszentmihalyi, M. (2002). *Flow: The Psychology of Happiness: The Classic Work on How to Achieve Happiness.* London: Random House.

Csikszmenthalyi, M. (2013). *Creativity: The Psychology of Discovery and Adventure.* New York: Harper Collins.

de Haan, E. (2008). *Relational Coaching: Journeys Towards Mastering One-to-one Learning.* Chichester: Wiley.

de Haan, E. (2012). *Supervision in Action.* Maidenhead: McGraw Hill.

de Haan, E., & Kasozi, A. (2015). Leaders in crisis: Attending to the shadow side. In L. Hall (ed.), *Coaching in Times of Crisis and Transformation: How to Help Individuals and Organisations Flourish.* London: Kogan Page. pp. 144–171.

de Haan, E., Bertie, C., Day, A., & Sills, C. (2010). Critical moments of clients and coaches: A direct-comparison study. *International Coaching Psychology Review, 5*(2), 109–128.

de Jong, A. (2010). Coaching ethics in the moment of choice. In J. Passmore (ed.), *Excellence in Coaching: The Industry Guide,* 2nd edn. London: Kogan Page. pp. 204–214.

Egan, G. (2013). *The Skilled Helper: A Problem Management and Opportunity Development Approach to Helping,* 10th edn. London: Cengage.

Endo, R. (1995). *Tao Shiatsu: Life Medicine for the 21st Century.* Tokyo: Tokyo Publications.

Erhard, W. H., & Jensen M. C. (2014). The four ways of being that create the foundation for great leadership, a great organisation and a great life. *Insigniam Quarterly* (quarterly.insigniam.com).

European Mentoring and Coaching Council (EMCC) (2017). EMCC Competence Framework. Available at www.emccouncil.org/webimages/EU/EIA/emcc-competence-framework-v2.pdf (accessed 23 November 2017).

European Mentoring and Coaching Council (EMCC) (2018). Global Code of Ethics for Coaches, Mentors and Supervisors. Available at https://emcc1.app.box.com/s/8s3tsveqieq6vr6n2itb0p9mpsxgcncd (accessed 6 November 2018).

Flores, F. (2012). *Conversations for Action and Collected Essays: Instilling a Culture of Commitment in Working Relationships.* North Charleston, SC: CreateSpace Independent Publishing Forum.

Fredrickson, B. (2001). The role of positive emotions in positive psychology: The broaden-and-build theory of positive emotions. *American Psychologist, 56,* 218–226.

Fredrickson, B. (2004). The broaden-and-build theory of positive emotions. *Philosophical Transactions of the Royal Society of London, 359,* 1367–1377.

French, J., & Raven, B. (1959). The bases of social power. In D. Cartwright (ed.), *Studies in Social Power.* Ann Arbor, MI: Institute for Social Research. pp. 150–167.

Fullan, M. (2004). *Leading in a Culture of Change: Personal Action Guide and Workbook.* San Francisco, CA: Wiley.

Gallwey, T. (1975). *Inner Game of Tennis*. London: Jonathan Cape.

Garvey, B. (2017). Foreword. In *Coaching Creativity: Transforming Your Practice*. Abingdon: Routledge.

Gash, J. (2017). *Coaching Creativity: Transforming Your Practice*. Abingdon: Routledge.

Ghate, D., Lewis, J., & Welbourn, D. (2013). Systems leadership: Exceptional leadership for exceptional times. Synthesis Paper, Executive Summary. Virtual Staff College, Nottingham.

Gilligan, C. (1982). *In a Different Voice: Psychological Theory and Women's Development*. Cambridge, MA: Harvard University Press.

Gillon, R. (1985). Autonomy and consent. In M. Lockwood (ed.), *Moral Dilemmas in Modern Medicine*. Oxford: Oxford University Press. pp. 7–22.

Green, S., McQuaid, M., Purtell, A., & Dulagil, A. (2017). The psychology of positivity at work. In L. Oades, M. Steger, A. Della Fave, & J. Passmore (eds), *The Psychology of Positivity and Strength-Based Approaches at Work*. Chichester: Wiley. pp. 11–33.

Grencavage, L. and Norcross, J. (1990). Where are the commonalities among the therapeutic common factors? *Professional Psychology: Research and Practice*, *21*(5): 372–8.

Hall, L. (2013). *Mindful Coaching: How Mindfulness Can Transform Coaching Practice*. London: Kogan Page.

Hardingham, A. (2004). *The Coach's Coach: Personal Development for Personal Developers*. London: Chartered Institute of Personnel and Development (CIPD).

Hawkins, P., & Smith, N. (2006). *Coaching, Mentoring and Organisational Consultancy: Supervision and Development*, 1st edn. Maidenhead: Open University Press.

Hawkins, P., & Smith, N. (2013). *Coaching, Mentoring and Organisational Consultancy: Supervision and Development*, 2nd edn. Maidenhead: Open University Press.

Hay, J. (2007). *Reflective Practice and Supervision for Coaches*. Maidenhead: Open University Press.

Hefferon, K., & Boniwell, I. (2011). *Positive Psychology: Theory, Research and Applications*. Maidenhead: Open University Press.

Heifetz, R. A., & Linsky, M. (2002). *Leadership on the Line: Staying Alive through the Dangers of Leading*. Boston, MA: Harvard Business School Press.

Heron, J. (1975). *Six-Category Intervention Analysis: Human Potential*. Research Project, University of Surrey.

Heron, J. (1999). *The Complete Facilitator's Handbook*. London: Kogan Page.

Heron, J. (2009). *Helping the Client: A Creative Practical Guide*, 3rd edn. London: Sage.

International Coach Federation (ICF) (2015). ICF Code of Ethics. Available at https://coachfederation.org/code-of-ethics (accessed 3 July 2018).

International Coach Federation (ICF) (2017). Core Competencies. Available at https://coachfederation.org/core-competencies (accessed 23 October 2017).

Iordanou, I. (2017). Making ethical decisions: An evaluation and a proposition. *Coaching at Work, 12,* 1.

Iordanou, I., Hawley, R., & Iordanou, C. (2017). *Values and Ethics in Coaching.* London: Sage.

Iyengar, S. (2010). *The Art of Choosing: The Decisions We Make Every Day: What They Say About Us and How We Can Improve Them.* London: Little, Brown.

Jowett, S., Kanakoglou, K., & Passmore, J. (2012). The application of the 3 + 1Cs relationship model in executive coaching. *Consulting Psychology Journal, 64*(3), 183–97.

Kahneman, D. (2011). *Thinking Fast and Slow.* London: Penguin Books.

Kandola, B. (2009). *The Value of Difference: Eliminating Bias in Organisations.* Oxford: Pearn Kandola.

Karpman, S. (2014). *A Game Free Life: The Drama Triangle and Compassion Triangle.* San Francisco, CA: Drama Triangle Publications.

Kaufman, J. C. (2009). *Creativity 101 (Psych 101).* New York: Springer.

Klein, G. (1998). *Sources of Power: How People Make Decisions* Cambridge, MA: MIT Press.

Kline, N. (1999). *Time to Think: Listening to Ignite the Human Mind.* London: Cassell.

Kowalski, R. (2011). *Mindfulness and Mind-balancing Handbook.* Milton Keynes: Speechmark Publishing.

Langer, E. (2005). *On Becoming an Artist: Reinventing Yourself Through Mindful Creativity.* New York: Ballantine Books.

Leary-Joyce, J. (2014). *Fertile Void: Gestalt Coaching at Work.* St Albans: AoEC Press.

Lee, G., & Roberts, I. (2010). Coaching for authentic leadership. In J. Passmore (ed.), *Leadership Coaching: Working with Leaders to Develop Elite Performance.* London: Kogan Page. pp. 17–34.

Lindqvist, S. (2002). *Exterminate All the Brutes.* London: Granta Books.

Lopez, S., Pedrotti, J., & Snyder, C. (2015). *Positive Psychology: The Scientific and Practical Explorations of Human Strengths,* 3rd edn. Thousand Oaks, CA: Sage.

Machin, S. (2010). The nature of the internal coaching relationship. *International Journal of Evidence-based Coaching and Mentoring,* Special Issue (4), 37–52.

MacKenzie, I. (2013). Mindfulness and presence in supervision. In E. Murdoch, & J. Arnold (eds). *Full Spectrum Supervision.* St. Albans: Panoma.

MacKie, D. (2016). *Strength-based Leadership Coaching in Organisations: An Evidence-based Guide to Positive Leadership Development.* London: Kogan Page.

Magyar-Moe, J., & Lopez, S. (2015). Strategies for accentuating hope. In S. Joseph (ed.), *Positive Psychology in Practice: Promoting Human Flourishing in Work, Health, Education, and Everyday Life,* 2nd edn. Chichester: Wiley. pp. 483–502.

Maister, D. H., Green, C. H., & Galford, R. M. (2002). *The Trusted Advisor.* London: Simon and Schuster.

Mattingly, C. (2005). Toward a vulnerable ethics of research practice. *Interdisciplinary Journal for Social Study of Health, Illness and Medicine, 9:* 453 – 471.

McGregor, C. (2015). *Coaching Behind Bars: Facing Challenges and Creating Hope in a Women's Prison*. Maidenhead: Open University Press.

McKenna, D., & Davis, S. (2009). Hidden in plain sight: The active ingredients of executive coaching. *Industrial and Organizational Psychology*, 2, 244–260.

Mehrabian, A. (1981). *Silent Messages: Implicit Communication of Emotions and Attitudes*. Belmont, CA: Wadsworth.

Miao, F., Koo, M., & Oishi, S. (2013). Subjective well-being. In S. David, I. Boniwell, & A. Conley-Ayers (eds), *The Oxford Handbook of Happiness*. Oxford: Oxford University Press. pp. 174–184.

Myers, D., & Myers, G. (2002). *Intuition: Its Powers and Perils*. New Haven, CT: Yale University Press.

Nevis, E. C. (2001). *Organisational Consulting: A Gestalt Approach*. Cambridge, MA: The Gestalt Institute of Cleveland Press.

O'Neill, M.B. (2007). *Coaching with Backbone and Heart: A Systems Approach to Engaging Leaders with their Challenges*, 2nd edn. San Francisco, CA: Jossey-Bass.

Passmore, J. (2015). *Excellence in Coaching: The Industry Guide to Best Practice*, 3rd edn. London: Kogan Page.

Passmore, J., & Turner, E. (2018). Reflections on integrity: The APPEAR model. *Coaching at Work*, 13, 2.

Passmore, J., Csigsas, Z., & Brown, H. (2017). *The state of play in European coaching and mentoring*. Report commissioned by the European Mentoring and Coaching Council and Henley Business School, University of Reading.

Patterson, E. (2011). Presence in coaching supervision. In J. Passmore (ed.), *Supervision in Coaching: Supervision, Ethics and Continuous Professional Development*. London: Kogan Page. pp. 117–137.

Perello, I. (2011). *Chasing the Light: Improving your Photography with Available Light*. Berkeley, CA: New Riders.

Peterson, C. (2006). *A Primer in Positive Psychology*. Oxford: Oxford University Press.

Peterson, C., & Seligman, M. E. P. (2004). *Character Strengths and Virtues: A Classification and Handbook*. Oxford: Oxford University Press.

Phillips, K. (2006). *Intuition in Coaching*. Handforth: Keri Phillips Associates.

Pink, D. (2005). *A Whole New Mind: Why Right-brainers Will Rule the World*. London: Marshall Cavendish.

Plaister-Ten, J. (2016). *The Cross-Cultural Coaching Kaleidoscope: A Systems Approach to Coaching Amongst Different Cultural Influences*. London: Karnac.

Rand, K., & Cheavens, J. (2009). Hope theory. In S. Lopez, & C. Snyder (eds), *The Oxford Handbook of Positive Psychology*, 2nd edn. Oxford: Oxford University Press. pp. 323–333.

Rath, T., & Harter, J. (2010). *Wellbeing: The Five Essential Elements*. New York: Gallup Press.

Ray, M., & Myers, R. (1986). *Creativity in Business.* New York, NY: Broadway.

Ridderstråle, J., & Nordström, K. (2004). *Karaoke Capitalism: Management for Mankind.* Harlow: Pearson Education/FT Prentice Hall.

Roam, D. (2008). *The Back of the Napkin: Solving Problems and Selling Ideas with Pictures.* London: Penguin.

Robinson, K. (2001). *Out of Our Minds: Learning to Be Creative.* Oxford: Capstone.

Rodenburg, P. (2009). *Presence: How to Use Positive Energy for Success in Every Situation.* London: Penguin.

Rogers, C. (1957). The necessary and sufficient conditions of therapeutic personality change. *Journal of Consulting Psychology, 21,* 95–103.

Rogers, C. (1961). *On Becoming a Person: A Therapist's View of Psychotherapy.* London: Constable.

Rogers, J. (2016). *Coaching Skills: The Definitive Guide to Being a Coach,* 4th edn. Maidenhead: Open University Press.

Ryan, R. M., & Deci, E. (2000). Self-determination theory and the facilitation of intrinsic motivation, self development and well-being. *American Psychologist, 55*(1), 68–78.

Scheier, M., & Carver, C. (1992). Effects of optimism on psychological and physical well-being: Theoretical overview and empirical update. *Cognitive Therapy and Research, 16,* 201–228.

Schwarz, D., & Davidson, A. (2009). *Facilitative Coaching: A Toolkit for Expanding Your Repertoire and Achieving Results.* San Francisco, CA: Pfeiffer.

Scrivener, J. (2005). *Learning Teaching: The Essential Guide to English Language Teaching.* Oxford: MacMillan.

Seignot, N. (2016). The ace up your sleeve. *Coaching at Work, 11*(5), 48–50.

Seligman, M. (1991). *Learned Optimism.* New York: Knopf.

Seligman, M. (2011). *Flourish: A New Understanding of Happiness and Wellbeing.* London: Nicholas Brealey.

Seligman, M., & Csikszentmihalyi, M. (2000). Positive psychology: An introduction. *American Psychologist, 55,* 5–14.

Sheather, A. (2017). Holding the space. *Coaching at Work, 12*(4), 48–50.

Sibbet, D. (2010). *Visual Meetings: How Graphics, Sticky Notes and Idea Mapping Can Transform Group Productivity.* Hoboken, NJ: Wiley.

Siegel, D. (2010). *The Mindful Therapist: A Clinician's Guide to Mindsight and Neural Integration.* New York, NY: Norton.

Sieler, A. (2018). Ontological coaching. In E. Cox, T. Bachkirova, & D. Clutterbuck (eds), *The Complete Handbook of Coaching,* 3rd edn. London: Sage. pp. 95–108.

Silsbee, D. (2008). *Presence-based Coaching: Cultivating Self-generative Leaders through Mind, Body and Heart.* San Francisco, CA: Jossey-Bass.

Simon, H. A. (1992). What is an explanation of behaviour? *Psychological Science, 3,* 150–161.

Spoth, J., Toman, S., Leichtman, R., & Allan, J. (2016). Gestalt approach. In J. Passmore, D.B. Peterson, & T. Freire (eds), *The Wiley Blackwell Handbook of the Psychology of Coaching and Mentoring*. Chichester: Wiley. pp. 385–406.

Steger, M. (2009). Meaning in life. In S. Lopez and C. Snyder (eds), *The Oxford Handbook of Positive Psychology*, 2nd edn. Oxford: Oxford University Press. pp. 679–687.

Stone, D., Patton, B. and Heen, S. (2000). *Difficult Conversations: How to Discuss What Matters Most*. London: Penguin Books.

Strozzi-Heckler, R. (2014). *The Art of Somatic Coaching: Embodying Skilful Action, Wisdom and Compassion*. Berkeley, CA: North Atlantic Books.

Theeboom, T., Beersma, B., & van Vianen, A. E. M. (2014). Does coaching work? A meta-analysis on the effects of coaching on individual level outcomes in an organizational context. *The Journal of Positive Psychology*, 9, 1–18.

Thompson, N. (2017). *Promoting Equality: Working with Diversity and Difference*, 4th edn. London: Palgrave.

Thomson, B. (2009). *Don't Just Do Something, Sit There: An Introduction to Non-directive Coaching*. Oxford: Chandos.

Tolle, E. (2011). *The Power of Now: A Guide to Spiritual Enlightenment*. London: Hodder and Stoughton.

Tourish, D. (2013). *The Dark Side of Transformational Leadership: A Critical Perspective*. Hove: Routledge.

van Nieuwerburgh, C. (2017). *An Introduction to Coaching Skills: A Practical Guide*, 2nd edn. London: Sage.

van Nieuwerburgh, C., Lomas, T., & Burke, J. (2018). Editorial. *Coaching: An International Journal of Theory, Research and Practice*, 11(2), 99–101.

Walumbwa, F. O. (2008). Authentic leadership: Development and validation of a theory-based measure. *Journal of Management*, 34, 89–126.

Ware, C. (2008). *Visual Thinking for Design*. Burlington, MA: Morgan Kaufman.

Wheatley, M. J., & Kelner-Rogers, M. (1996). *A Simpler Way*. San Francisco, CA: Berrett-Koehler.

Whitmore, J. (1992). *Coaching for Performance: A Practical Guide to Growing Your Own Skills*. London: Nicholas Brealey.

Whitmore, J. (2009). *Coaching for Performance: GROWing Human Potential and Purpose*. 4th edn. London: Nicholas Brealey.

Whitmore, J. (2017). *Coaching for Performance: The Principles and Practice of Coaching and Leadership*, 5th edn. London: Nicholas Brealey.

Whittington, J. (2016). *Systemic Coaching and Constellations: An Introduction to the Principles, Practices and Application*, 2nd edn. London: Kogan Page.

Whyte, D. (2015). *Consolations: The Solace, Nourishment and Underlying Meaning of Everyday Words*. Langley, WA: Many Rivers Press.

Williams, M., & Penman, D. (2011). *Mindfulness: A Practical Guide to Finding Peace in a Frantic World*. London: Piatkus.

Wilson, C. (2014). *Performance Coaching: A Complete Guide to Best Practice Coaching and Training*, 2nd edn. London: Kogan Page.

Zimbardo, P. G., & Boyd, J. N. (1999). Putting time in perspective: A valid, reliable individual-differences metric. *Journal of Personality and Social Psychology, 77*, 1271–1288.

INDEX